At a gala opening at the old Loewe's Sheridan on May 29, 1946, Lucille Ball enthused to her fervent admirers, "The Village is the greatest place in the World."

Grove Street, 1934. (Note the price of an apartment on building at left)—Anthony Lanz

THE PICTURE BOOK OF GREENWICH VILLAGE

WRITTEN AND COMPILED BY R. BRUCE GAYLORD

Special thanks to Geoff Brown, Marian Connolly and Leonard Grarisco for their assistance on the first edition manuscripts, and to the Jefferson Market Branch of the New York Public Library.

This edition is dedicated to William Acker, Photographer and Friend.

A CITADEL PRESS BOOK
Published by Carol Publishing Group

First Carol Publishing Group Edition 1991

A Citadel Press Book
Published by Carol Publishing Group
Citadel Press is a registered trademark of
Carol Communications, Inc.

Editorial Offices   Sales & Distribution Offices
600 Madison Avenue   120 Enterprise Avenue
New York, NY 10022   Secaucus, NJ 07094

In Canada: Musson Book Company
A division of General Publishing Co. Limited
Don Mills, Ontario

Manufactured in the United States of America
10 9 8 7 6 5 4 3 2 1

Carol Publishing Group books are available at special discounts
for bulk purchases, for sales promotions, fund raising, or
educational purposes. Special editions can also be created to
specifications. For details contact: Special Sales Department,
Carol Publishing Group, 120 Enterprise Ave., Secaucus, NJ 07094

ISBN 0-8065-1236-9

Front cover: A model of the current Washington Arch—made of wood and staff (plaster)—was built on 8th Street and Fifth Avenue to celebrate the hundredth anniversary of George Washington's inauguration.   April 30, 1989. (UPI/Bettmann Newsphotos)

Back cover: A view of Washington Park taken in the late 1920s. (UPI/Bettmann Newsphotos)

"I was under no illusion that the Village was any longer in its great days—I knew that in the matter of residential preference I was a mere epigone. So much so, indeed, that my apartment was not in a brownstone or in a more-or-less reconditioned tenement, but in a brand-new, yellow-brick, jerry-built six-story apartment building...Still the Village was the Village, there seemed no other place in New York where a right-thinking person might live..."

Lionel Trilling

"Baptizing Scene" 1834. On the right stands Fort Gansevoort, one of a series of forts erected by the Federal Government after the burning of Washington D.C. Christened "The White Fort" by local residents, it was named for Colonel Peter Gansevoort. a hero of the British and Indian onslaught against Fort Schuyler in 1777. His grandson, Herman Melville, worked on the family wharf at the foot of Gansevoort Street from 1866 to 1885 after becoming disillusioned by criticism of his writing. The fort was demolished in 1849 when landfill between Perry and Fourteenth west of Washington Street erased the contours of the bay and the little spur of land where Fort Gansevoort and the original Indian village of Sapokanikan once stood.

THE HISTORY OF GREENWICH VILLAGE

The late summer sun touched the round bark houses and wooden lean-tos of the tiny village of Sapokanikan, which perched in solitude on the palisades overlooking the broad Mahicanittuk river. A small group of Canarsee Indians came every year to this landing spot on the west side of Manhattan Island to harvest the famous tobacco that gave this village its name.

The Canarsee tribe ranged over the marshes of lower Manhattan and eastward across present-day Brooklyn to Jamaica Bay. Upper Manhattan was at that time controlled by the warrior tribe of Weckquaesgeek, whose sachem, Rechewac, had his main headquarters close to what is now 94th Street and Park Avenue. The latter group had been forced down from upstate New York by ongoing warfare with the Mohicans.

But in 1609 the area in general, and particularly Lower Manhattan was at peace. Two sleepy villages, Sapokanikan on the west and Wepoes ("rabbit ground") on the East River near present Canal Street, were the only permanent settlements and by mutual agreement the various tribes had set aside the very tip of Manhattan as a neutral trading ground. It was probably from here that the first sighting of Henry Hudson's *De Halve Moon* was made by the much-awed natives.

The history of Manhattan began when Hudson anchored his "yacht" off the battery on the afternoon of September 12, 1609. The simple natives who probably watched from Sapokanikan as he sailed up the river on his way to the future site of Fort Orange (Albany), could not have suspected the far-reaching effects of this first Dutch "invasion"

The following sixty years saw the arrival of a sufficient number of colonists to displace all of the natives on lower Manhattan and most of Staten Island.

Hudson returned twice from Holland before he was killed in an Indian attack at Fort Orange and his partner Adriaen Block found himself reluctantly responsible for the first settlement on Manhattan, when his ship "The Tiger" burned offshore in 1614. They erected temporary huts near the Battery while they built a new ship.

The first permanent settlers (30 families of Walloons) were sent to Fort Orange in 1624 by the newly formed Dutch West India Company, and Manhattan was officially settled in 1626. On May 4th of that year Peter Minuit became governor of *Niew Amsterdam*. That summer he sent the first shipment of American goods to Amsterdam, Holland. It consisted of "7,146 beaver skins, 675 otter skins, 48 mink, 36 wild cat and various other sorts along with many pieces of oak timber and hickory."

The history of Greenwich Village actually began in Holland, when a nephew of the powerful patroon, Kilian Van Rensselaer, wangled the job of Director of New Amsterdam, along with "a little piece of land."

Prior to Henry Hudson's landing, an Italian captain in the service of France, Verrazano, had in 1524 explored the upper and lower bays of Manhattan. Then, in 1550 Estevan Gomez, a Portugese flying the flag of Charles V of Spain, probably stopped nearby. And in 1570, Jean Cossin of Dieppe produced extensive charts showing he also had visited the harbor vicinity. All of this prior activity was multi-national exploration only; it was the Englishman Henry Hudson's sailing on behalf of the Dutch Crown that brought the contact that first established a colony.

At this time it was the habit of these empire builders to divide the colony's lands into farms or *Bouweries,* and give powerful and/or deserving people a portion of this land. As soon as the acquisitive Wouter Van Twiller (the nephew) became director in March, 1633, he deeded one of these farms (with tobacco already growing on it) to himself, and called it the *Bossen Bouwerie,* or farm in the woods. It stretched from present day Christopher to Twenty-First Streets and from approximately Fifth Avenue to the North or Hudson River. (The reason that old property boundaries are so difficult to presently establish is that they were determined by natural obstacles, such as a creek or hills.)

In 1635 while Van Twiller was happily deeding most of Staten Island and many small islands around Manhattan to himself, a house was erected for him at Sopokanikan. Houses for farm workers and servants inevitably followed and the *Dutch* Village of *Sopokanikanee* or *Noortwyck* was born. (Mention of the Village was first made in 1653).

Below present Christopher Street a grant was made in 1636 to Anneke Jans after Van Twiller had been recalled to Holland. Buildings were erected and the parameters of the future Greenwich Village was complete.

The relative calm that had pervaded the area since Peter Miniut had "purchased" Manhattan Island from Meijeterma and Seyseys (two chiefs at the Indian village Werpoes), turned to out and out warfare with the appointment of William Kieft as Director-General on September 2, 1637.

The Dutch tended to look askance at the *Willden* (Indians) and more than once had been outright vicious. The Reverend Jonas Michaelius, first Dutch Reformed dominie to arrive at New Amsterdam expressed a decidedly un-Christian attitude towards the natives when he wrote; "As to the natives of this country, I find them entirely savage and wild, strangers to all decency, yes, uncivil and stupid as garden poles, proficient in all wickedness and godlessness; devilish men, who serve nobody but the Devil, that is, the spirit which in their language they call Menetto; under which title they comprehend everything that is subtle and crafty and beyond human skill and power. They have so much witchcraft, divination, sorcery and wicked arts that they can hardly be held in by bands or locks. They are thievish and treacherous as they are tall; and in cruelty they are altogether inhuman, more than barbarous, far exceeding the Africans." And the bellecose Mr. Kieft put these feelings into action.

The Weckquasgecks of upper Manhattan had never made any treaties with the Dutch. The dealings of the Carnarsee tribe of lower Manhattan had no effect on them at all. Relations were at best strained and when on March 3, 1639 the sale of powder and lead to the Indians (on which they had come to rely) was prohibited and Kieft and his council had resolved to exact from them a tribute in maize, furs or wampum, by force if

These three photos are the *Half Moon* in Holland before leaving for New York.

Brown Bros.

Underwood & Underwood

Underwood & Underwood

*I*n 1909, on the 300th anniversary of the discovery of Manhattan by Henry Hudson, the city fathers in cooperation with Dutch officials decided to construct an exact duplicate of the original *Half Moon* and sail it from Amsterdam to New York. Here it was the centerpiece of a weeklong celebration which was heralded as "the coming great event which for the next few weeks will obsess the interest of patriotic citizens in all sections of our country. More than 5,000,000 visitors will swoop down on 'Little Old New York' and help to commemorate the 300th anniversary of Hendrik Hudson's map changing discovery of the river which now bears his name and the epoch making trip of the *Clermont* when Robert Fulton sailed the first steamboat up this river about 200 years later."

The *Half Moon* anchored off Greenwich Village, 1909.

PROGRAMME
OF THE
HUDSON-FULTON CELEBRATION

The programme of events for the Hudson-Fulton celebration, which will begin on Saturday, September 25, and last until October 3, and on that day shift to the upper Hudson towns and cities, is as follows:

SATURDAY, SEPTEMBER 25.

The American and foreign naval vessels will rendezvous in New York harbor, and will be one of ten squadrons. The first will consist of ocean-going and coastwise merchant vessels; then will come steamboats plying in inland waters of the United States, including ferryboats; steam yachts, commanded by W. Butler Duncan, Jr., will be next in line, followed by motor boats under the command of J. Adolph Mollenhauer. The fifth squadron will be made up of tugs and steam lighters, followed by the sixth, consisting of sailing craft. Police boats and the craft devoted to the preservation of the public safety, such as wrecking, fire and hospital boats, will make up the seventh squadron, and then will come the escort squadron, including such Government craft as torpedo boats and submarines, naval militia vessels, steam launches, and cutters in the Government service, escorting the Half Moon and the Clermont, under the command of Commander R. P. Forshew of the Second Battalion of the Naval Militia. The patrol squadron, the ninth by number, is to be made up of vessels in the revenue service and other Government, State or private vessels authorized by the War Department to do patrol duty. The final squadron will be the scout squadron, and will consist of fast steamers and motor boats detailed to do dispatch boat duty.

At 10.30 a. m. the escort squadron will assemble with the replicas of the Half Moon and Clermont off Constable Point, in the Kill von Kull, will manoeuvre with them along the Staten Island and Bay Ridge shores. The formation of the various other squadrons will begin between 12.30 and 1 o'clock, and at 1.15 the whole fleet will start up the bay to the Hudson River, the escort division, with the replicas of the Half Moon and Clermont in the center.

The fleet will steam slowly up to Forty-second street, then pass to the west between the war vessels and the Jersey shore, the warship line extending to 175th street — its northern end. Then it will recross the river and head downstream on the New York side to 110th street. There the official reception of the Half Moon and Clermont will be celebrated with appropriate ceremonies.

---

ii   *HUDSON-FULTON CELEBRATION.*

The head of the parade will reach 110th street about 4 o'clock. In the evening the same parade will be repeated, starting at 7.30 o'clock, amid a brilliant display of fireworks.

MONDAY, SEPTEMBER 27.

There will be a general decoration of public and private buildings from New York to the head of the Hudson River. The day will begin with a reception to the official guests at the headquarters of the Department of the East, on Governor's Island.

TUESDAY, SEPTEMBER 28.

The special feature will be the historic parade in the City of New York, participated in by people of all nationalities. The procession will be composed of floats and moving tableaux representing the principal events in the history of the aboriginal, the Dutch, the English, the Revolutionary, and the American periods of our history.

The parade will start at a time to be announced at 110th street and Central Park West, will proceed down Central Park West to Fifty-ninth street, thence through to Fifth avenue, and down to Twenty-third street. From Fifth avenue and Twenty-third street the parade will either proceed down to Washington Square, to disband at Fourth street, or else will turn up Madison avenue a few blocks, and then disband.

In the evening there will be the official literary exercises in the Metropolitan Opera House and the Brooklyn Academy of Music, at which men of national and international prominence will make addresses.

WEDNESDAY, SEPTEMBER 29.

This will be essentially a historical day, designed to be participated in by universities, colleges, schools, museums, and learned and patriotic societies throughout the State.

There will be commemorative exercises at Columbia University, New York University, the College of the City of New York, Cooper Union, St. John's University, Fordham, the Brooklyn Institute of Arts and Sciences, all the public schools and nearly all the private institutions of learning throughout the State.

There will also be motorboat races and aquatic sports on the Hudson River. The crews of many of the warships will take part in these contests. Fifteen thousand dollars will be spent for prizes of various kinds. The preliminaries of the motorboat races will be held on Saturday, Monday and Tuesday, and the finals on Wednesday, at a point approximately off Ninety-sixth street.

At the same time up-river there will be high power motor boat races at Yonkers, and sailing races for 30-footers and classes below at Newburg, including possibly the American and Dutch challengers in the International Sonder Class races.

HUDSON-FULTON CELEBRATION

THURSDAY, SEPTEMBER 30.

The military parade. This parade will include fully 25,000 men of the United States Army and Navy, the National Guard, the Naval Militia, various veteran organizations, and landing parties from the foreign warships. It will follow the same route as the historical parade of Tuesday. Only the military and naval organizations mentioned will march, and no civic organizations will have place in the line.

FRIDAY, OCTOBER 1.

The naval parade up-river, with incidental ceremonies along the line. The great fleet, organized into three squadrons, will start at the hours of 8, 9 and 10 o'clock, or else 7, 8 and 9 o'clock, as may be thought best, to escort the Half Moon and the Clermont up river as far as Newburgh Bay. That is as far as it will be practicable for some of the naval vessels to go.

At Newburg there will be elaborate festivities. The Half Moon and the Clermont will be turned over to an up-river squadron, which will take the replicas on to Albany. The historical parade will be repeated in Brooklyn.

SATURDAY, OCTOBER 2.

A general carnival day for New York City. In all the cities along the Hudson carnival exercises will take place, participated in by the children. On the Stony Point battlefield the Daughters of the Revolution will unveil their Memorial Arch.

In the evening there will be one great carnival parade, with moving allegorical tableaux, participated in by the German societies.

Every municipal building and thousands of private buildings, every great bridge spanning the East River, every monument, and many of the great thoroughfares will be illuminated with tens of thousands of electric lights. There will be 14,000 of these on the Queensboro Bridge and nearly as many on each of the other great bridges. Along the Hudson River front there will be an illumination of both sides of the river from Spuyten Duyvil to Seventy-second street.

On Riverside Drive there will be two enormous batteries of searchlights, one located at 110th street, with twelve searchlights aggregating 1,700,000 candle power, and another of four searchlights, aggregating 400,000 candle power, which will be turned upon Grant's Tomb. Meantime there will be special firework displays on floats along the river front in honor of the visiting fleets.

At 9 o'clock the signal fires will be lighted all along the Hudson. The points selected are Governor's Island, Fort Lee, Fort Washington, Spuyten Duyvil, Alpina, Hasting's Point, Dunderburgh, Anthony's Nose, Sugar Loaf Hill, West Point, Constitution Island, Storm King, Bull Hill, and Crow's Nest.

It has been arranged that President Taft shall give the signal for lighting all these fires. When the signal is given rockets, bombs, and an

Three pages from the Hudson—Clermont Celebration programme. Note that the parades came down Fifth Avenue to Washington Square.

necessary, the Indian Wars began.

To exaserbate the situation an army of Mohicans from the upper Hudson Valley declared war on the Weckquasgecks of Manhattan and New Jersey in February of 1643. Caught between two hostile groups, the Weckquasgecks fled away from their age old enemies, towards the Dutch.

Misreading the situation and probably uncaring for all except action, Kieft ordered his forces to attack the Indians at their temporary encampments at Pavonia (New Jersey). The Dutch massacred about 120 Indians(mostly women and children)and touched off a bloody war that lasted until an uneasy settlement was reached on August 30, 1645.

During this, all outlying villages were under constant threat of attacks and many on Staten Island were sacked and burned.

Kieft was recalled early in 1646 and perished at sea before reaching Holland.

On July 28th of that year, Petrus Stuyvesant was appointed Governor of the colony.Under his rule the Dutch demeanor towards the Indians was not improved and in fact on 1655 they attacked again (after the murder of a Indian woman on Manhattan) killing 100 of the Dutch and capturing 150 more while laying waste to the Bouweries of Pavonia and Hoboken.

The wars with the Indians subsided just as Holland went to war with England. In 1664, with the English victory assured, King Charles II granted to his brother James, the Duke of York, "a part of Maine, all of Long Island, Marthas's Vineyard and all the land from the west side of the Connecticut River to the east side of Delaware Bay. From August 29th to September 8th of that year, New Amsterdam was surrendered by Stuyvesant to Colonel Richard Niccols of the British Army, who changed the city's name to New York.

At this time, the land north of the present Fourteenth Street was for all practical purposes, virgin territory. Even as late as 1679 when Danckaerts and Skuyler, the Labadist missionaries who walked over much of Manhattan Island, stopped at the village of Sapokanikan, wolves were still plentiful enough for the City Council to declare a bounty on them. The more humane attitude of the British(in this area)towards the Indians had erased most worries of attack by 1700.

Although the area miles out of the city was commonly referred to as "Greenwich" at this time - the first official mention occurs in 1721 deed that refers to "the Bossen Bouerie, alias Greenwich."

In 1733 a British Admiral, Sir Peter Warren, moved onto a part of the old Bossen Bouwerie. This was a fine estate (or country seat, as it was called at that time), some 300 acres that stretched from the Hudson River to what is now Fifth Avenue and from Third Street to 21st Street. The Warren house was a square farm building with large chimneys at either end and a widow's walk on the roof. It sat on a hill which would now be bounded by Charles, Perry, Bleecker and West

SIR PETER WARREN K.B.
Vice Admiral of the Red Squadron.

Admiral Sir Peter Warren first arrived in New York City in 1728. He married Susanna de Lancey, daughter of one of the oldest families in New York and purchased his estate in Greenwich in 1733. They had three daughters: Charlotte who married Willoughby, Earl of Abingdon; Ann, who became the Baroness of Southhampton when she wed Charles Fitzroy and Susanna, the only one who wed for love, to Colonel Otis Skinner. Streets and roads were named after all son-inlaws but only Abingdon Square remains. Sir Peter was much favored by both the British and American governments. Although he gained much of his wealth from the booty of war, he was both "kind to his men as well as to the prisoners". He became a member of parliament, retired to England before the Revolution leaving his estate to be divided among his children and was finally buried in a place of honor in Westminster Abbey. His eulogy was written by Dr. Samuel Johnson.

Fourth Streets. Several streets in the Village were named after members of Warren's family, but Abindgon Square (named for his daughter's husband) is the only one that survives. The Admiral himself is remembered by Warren Street, south of Canal.

The Admiral was a man of considerable wealth and the warmth of his hospitality was well known. On the front table of his spacious hall, for example, there was always a basket of sponge cake, baked fresh daily for any visitor who dropped by, and the Warrens' annual party for Greenwich children, with a gift for each child, was an exciting event.

For more than a century and a quarter the Warren house was the most important dwelling on this portion of the island. It was the nucleus about which other country seats clustered—including, before 1767, those of William Bayard, James Jouncey and Oliver De Lancey, Lady Warren's brother.

Winding lanes, later the thoroughfares of a thriving community, led to the river's bank, and children swam and fished in the sparkling water that lapped up on a narrow, sandy beach. In winter there was sledding on the hillsides and skating on the frozen Lispenard Meadows further south, now the site of Canal Street.

The Washington Square we see today was a marsh. Minetta Brook emptied into a swamp at Charlton and West Houston Streets. Minetta Brook has been covered over for years, but true Villagers choose to believe it still bubbles away underground. The legend has been encouraged from time to time when land has been excavated for building. In 1950, the press reported that the little stream was threatening the foundations of the New York University Law School, then under construction, but alas, such optimism was unfounded.

In 1705, Queen Anne granted 62 acres to Trinity Church between Fulton and Christopher Streets. On part of this property, near what is now Charlton and Varick Streets, a mansion was erected in 1767 which would become the most famous in all old New York. It was built by Major Abraham Mortier, a leading merchant and Commissary of the King's Troops, who acquired the land on a 99-year lease from the Church. It was called Richmond Hill.

In 1776 George Washington made Richmond Hill his headquarters. It was there on September 12th of that year that he and his Council of General Officers voted to evacuate New York and planned their Long Island campaign.

When New York City became the temporary capital of the United States in 1789, Richmond Hill renewed its reputation for hospitality. Vice President John Adams and his family moved into the house and, according to letters Mrs. Adams wrote, enjoyed a number of happy years there. Mrs. Adams wrote her sister, "In front of the house, the noble Hudson rolls his majestic waves, and bearing upon his bosom innumerable small vessels, which are constantly forwarding the rich products of the neighboring soil to the busy hand of a more extensive commerce...On the left, the city opens upon us, intercepted only by clumps of trees, and some rising ground, which serves to heighten the beauty of the scene, by appearing to conceal a part."

When the capital was moved to Philadelphia, the Adams family moved also, and in 1794 Richmond Hill became the home of Aaron Burr. Burr, then a United States Senator, was a brilliant lawyer and a leading Jeffersonian Republican (the Democrats of that day). At Richmond Hill he was host to such figures as Thomas Jefferson, James Madison and foreign visitors James Bonaparte, Tallyrand, and Louis Philippe, later King of France. (Burr's remarkable daughter Theodosia assumed the arduous task of hostess, although she was only 14.)

Burr lived here in splendor until that Friday in July, 1804, when he crossed the river to Weehawken, to meet Alexander Hamilton in their fateful duel.The first shot spelled death for Hamilton, but it also ended the career of the clever, suave, unscrupulous man who was Vice President of the United States--and would have been President, had it not been for the antagonism of Hamilton.

The wounded Hamilton was rowed back to the village, where he died in the home of William Bayard. The site of Bayard's country estate on the river front in Upper Greenwich is traditionally placed at 82 Jane Street although the house was probably located in the middle of the block between Jane and Horatio Streets.

Burr fled from Richmond Hill. The lease on the estate, which he held on long terms from Trinity Church, was sold by his creditors to John Jacob Astor.

Since Greenwich was on higher ground than the southern end of the island, and because of its verdant fields, woodlands and flowing brooks, it was considered a healthful area and provided a relaxing atmosphere in which to live. Prosperous merchants and businessmen of the day built summer homes for their families there, and as time went on chose to live in the "suburbs" year round to escape the increasing noise and filth of the commercial district in lower Manhattan.

And so, in the late 1700's, the Village, pastoral and calm, was a quiet, pleasant place. But the pace in the rapidly growing city began to accelerate.

Ships landing in lower New York harbor in increasing numbers brought many tempting things from abroad; they also brought yellow fever, smallpox and cholera. Coupled with the appalling lack of sanitation in the city, epidemics became common.

Although not yet identified, the many deaths from the fever recorded in 1658 and the epidemic in the summer of 1703 when "mortality was so considerable that the inhabitants fled to the country for safety" were most certainly yellow fever. Everyone who could afford it scattered to the outlying villages during the late sum-

The engraving at right appeared in the 1884 edition of Janvier's New York. Weehawken Street was cut through the grounds of the old State Prison prior to 1834. One house remains (unprotected by Landmark status) from that era at No. 8, built by George F. Munson, boat builder.

Weehawken Street.

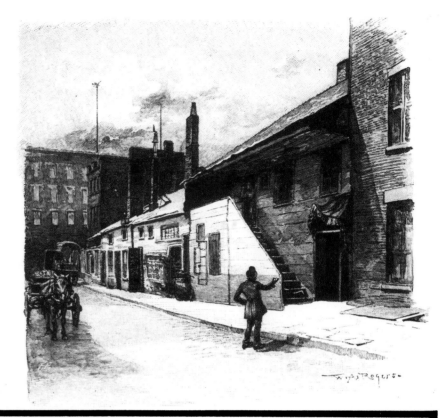

This house was erected prior to 1775

Hull's Stage in 1842

mer. It became official as early as April 18, 1739 in a letter to the Duke of Newcastle from Lt. Governor Clarke. He began: "I beg leave to inform your Grace, that, the small pox being in town, and one third part of the Assembly not having had it, I gave them leave to sit at Greenwich, a small village about two or three miles out of town." The Assembly returned to houses at the end of Greenwich Lane in the summers of 1742 and 1743 when there was "a malignant epidemic strongly resembling the yellow-fever in type" which caused more than two hundred deaths in the city proper.

But the most severe "fever summers" occured in the last decade of the Eighteenth and the first forty years of the Nineteenth Century.

The first in 1791 caused relatively few deaths; the second in 1795 killed nearly seven hundred; and the epidemic of 1798 claimed more than two thousand victims and paralyzed the city. While the panic lasted, not only Greenwich but all the towns and villages in the greater New York area were crowded with refugees. (A death of one of its employees at this time prompted the Bank of New York to buy property on a country lane in Greenwich and locate a branch there during the ensuing summers. As other institutions joined it, the lane became known as "the street of banks" and officially became Bank Street in 1807.)

But the worst was yet to come. David Devoe remarks in his *Market Place* (published in 1850) that the "yellow fever outbreaks in 1798, 1799, 1803, and 1805 tended to much increase the formation of a village near the Spring Street Market and one also near the State Prison," but the ferocity of the epidemic of the summer 1822 built up many streets with numerous wooden buildings.

Many citizens began to leave the city as early as June, but even increasing fatalities from the fever could not convince the Common Council (comprised for the most part of influential businessman) to close down commerce and recognize the seriousness of this epidemic. It was not until the first week in August that the Council faced reality, ordered all persons from their homes and declared the area below City Hall an "infected district." Only the black slaves, who were largely unaffected by the fever, and the very poor remained.

Hardie gives the following vivid picture of the exodus: "Saturday the 24th August, our city presented the apearance of a town beseiged. From daybreak till night one line of carts, containing boxes, merchandise, and effects, were seen moving towards Greenwich Village and the upper parts of the city. Carriages and hacks, wagons and horsemen were scouring the streets (with lime); persons with anxiety strongly marked on their countenances and with hurried gait, were hustling through the streets. Temporary stores and offices were erected, and even on the ensuing day (Sunday) carts were in motion, and the saw and hammer busily at work."

In September Colonel W. L. Stone, editor of the New York Commercial Advertiser, wrote to his wife,

"you cannot conceive the distressing situation we are in, and the whole town, the fever is worse every hour. I saw the hearse pass the office an hour ago with seven more sick on it. Thus the dead are carried to the grave, and the sick out of town—to die—on the same melancholy carriages.". Later he continued about the Yellow Fever epidemic" a severe nipping frost I have no doubt will check it and even yet I hope that we shall be able to remove back (i.e. from Greenwich) by the first of next month."

To accomodate the refugees builders threw together everything from ramshackle huts south of Washington Square to huge boarding houses in the West Village. The Reverend Mr. Marselus wrote that "he saw corn growing on the present corner of Hammond (West Eleventh) and Fourth Streets on a Saturday morning, and on the following Monday Sykes & Niblo had a house erected capable of accomodating three hundred boarders. Even the Brooklyn ferry-boats ran up here (the foot of Christopher Street) daily."

Business and government offices such as the Customs House, the Post Office, insurance companies and printers of newspapers relocated their offices in the area. When the winter frosts ended the scourge, many of the refugees returned home and abandoned the wooden buildings they had erected as emergency shelter. Virtually all the lanes and "regulated streets" (those graded to level according to the Commissioners Plan of 1807-11) in Greenwich Village had many houses on them became permanent homes and offices as the population quadrupled between 1825 and 1860.

The foot of 10th Street on the river had been chosen as the site for a State Prison. According to the

The State Prison located at the foot of West Tenth Street near the Hudson River. The city of Manhattan was still clustered mainly around the tip of the island and when prisoners were arraigned and sentenced near the Battery they were taken by barge upriver to the prison. Thus came into the language the phrase "to be sent up the river" now a universal euphemism for being sent to prison.

respected historian Janvier, "The prison was opened November 28, 1797, when seventy prisoners were transferred thither, and it continued in use a little more than thirty years. The male prisoners were transferred to Sing Sing in 1828 and the female prisoners in the spring of 1829—when the entire property was sold into private hands." Unlike what we might expect today, this development was not greeted with dismay. Rather, residents took great pride in the institution and described it as "pleasant and airy" and modern in the concept of teaching trades to both male and female inmates.

An important result of the building of the prison and the establishment of government and commercial offices in Greenwich Village was that the Hull's Line stagecoach began making five round trips daily from the Greenwich Hotel on the waterfront to Federal Hall downtown.

Another new center of activity was the Greenwich Market, which opened in 1812 on Christopher Street near the river. A substantial produce market, it brought farmers from Weehawken across the river, and the short street where they unloaded their fresh New Jersey vegetables still bears that name.

This street may have been in existence near the cove at the foot of Skinner road (Christopher) as early as 1775, and it was definitely marked in early property maps when the city bought the site of the State Prison. A slight jog in the prison property was indicated when they built around this street. One house from that period   remains, which makes it without a doubt, the oldest extant structure in Greenwich Village!

The market also brought tradesmen to the area. Weavers, sailmakers, carters and butchers were among

The streets of Greenwich followed for the most part at that time the established routes of earlier lanes or adhered to the lines marking property boundaries. But now the rumblings of progress were heard faintly in the distance: early in the 19th century, the City's Commissioners (1807-11) schemed to overlay the undeveloped land on the entire island with a huge grid of north and south-bound avenues and east and west-bound streets. The system was not well received generally, and nowhere was opposition quite so vociferous as in Greenwich Village. Apparently unable to sway the aroused Villagers, the staid city fathers spread their grid over the land to the east and the north, for the most part avoiding the Village proper.

the new residents, plying their trades close to the Hudson and building their rustic little houses in groups of twos and threes.

By the 1820's row-house construction had swept into the westermost section of the Village. In 1817 John Jacob Astor bought a six-acre tract owned by Aaron Burr. The mansion on it (Richmond Hill) was moved to the southeast corner of Charlton and Varick Streets and its promontory namesake leveled. Astor followed Burr's original map and plan. The property was divided into standard twenty-five-foot by one-hundred-foot building lots and sold to local architect builders. Nearly all the surviving federal houses in the present Charlton-King-Vandam Historic District were not built by individuals as family residences but solely by speculators.

The area at the foot of Christopher Street near the State Prison and Christopher Market began to rapidly expand toward Astor"s development at Varick Street. Federal style row houses filled the streets and lanes on the northern portion of the Trinity Church property (62 acres which ended at Christopher Street) that had been granted in 1705 by Queen Anne to the Church.

In contrast, that portion of the Village near Fifth Avenue was largely unpopulated. Only about 15 families lived near the Sand Hill Road (Eighth Street). A few families lived near the present Minetta Lane and farm buildings on the Herring and Bleecker and Brevoort estates were the only permanent buildings. (Legend has it that in 1807 old man Brevoort chased city surveyors off his property with a blunderbuss when they attempted to put Eleventh Street through his favorite orchard. In fact, the street has not been put through to this day and Broadway bends around the former site of his orchard, a mute reminder of one man's victory over "progress.")

The site of Washington Square was still a marsh threaded by Minetta Brook in 1789 when the city purchased half of it for a potter's field from the Herring family. Eight years later another portion (to the west of Minetta Brook which ran about fifty feet west of our present arch) was acquired from Colonel William S. Smith, an officer of Washington's army. One last thin strip was later bought from the Warren estate to complete the dimensions of Washington Square. Not only was this site used to bury unknown or unclaimed dead, but it was the site of public gallows. (When Lafayette visited in 1824 he was treated to the sight of no less than twenty highwaymen hanged by the neck.)

In 1828, however, the area was drained, the gallows torn down, some bodies exhumed and buried elsewhere, and the Square was designated as the Washington Military Parade Ground. Within the next 10 years, the houses on the north side of the Square were built. Known as "The Row," they were the most fashionable in New York City. Occasionally residents of the Row were reminded of the Square's less-than-aristocractic past. E.N. Tailer, who had lived at No. 11

New York University's original Gothic Revival building (1837) was demolished in 1894. Henry James wrote its requiem in The American Scene; "The grey and more or less hallowed University building—wasn't it somehow with a desperate bravery, both castellated and gabled?—has vanished from the earth, and vanished with it the two or three adjacent houses, of which my birth place was one."

Washington Square North in the late 1830's wrote "I remember when heavy guns were drawn over the Square, after it became a parade ground, that the weight broke through the ground into the trenches in which the dead were buried and crushed the tops of some of the coffins.. At one time near Fourth and Thompson Street, I saw a vault under the sidewalk opened and the body found there was still wrapped in yellow sheets in which the yellow fever victims were buried."

New York University (founded in 1834) erected a fine Gothic Revival Building on the northeast corner of the Square in 1837, the first in a conclave which would eventually surround most of the Square. The stones for its construction were cut by Sing Sing convicts, which caused the first mass labor demonstrations, organized by the stone cutters guild. The building was completed only after the demonstrators were cleared out by the 27th regiment of the New York National Guard, a move approved by the community.

Between 1840 and 1870 many wonderful mansions and townhouses were built along lower Fifth Avenue. No. 24 was the splendid Greek Revival mansion of Henrik Brevoort, and on the eastern side of the Avenue stood the Brevoort Hotel, which sadly was demolished in the early 1900's. Famous visitors to the hotel included Jenny Lind, "The Swedish Nightingale," Edward VII, then Prince of Wales, and Caruso.

During this period two famous churches were erected on Fifth Avenue. The First Presbyterian Church (1845), at 11th Street, was modeled after a church in Bath, England, and remains to this day, surrounded by lovely gardens. The Church of the Ascension (1841), at 10th Street, included many wealthy families among its parishioners. It was here in 1844 that the wedding of then-President John Tyler and Julia Gardiner took place. (She was a descendant of the family to whom Gardiner's Island—off Long Island—had been deeded by the King of England in 1668.)

Nearby, at Broadway and East 10th Street, Grace Church was erected in 1846.

William Rhinelander Stewart, who arrived in New York in the 1840's, conceived the idea of placing a triumphal arch on Washington Square. Through his effort and those of many others, a temporary arch was built across Fifth Avenue in 1889. Public demands for a permanent structure was satisfied when the cornerstone for Stanford Whites famous marble arch was laid in 1895.

Prior to the Civil War the Village went through a period of great expansion. Construction of row houses continued until about 1860, at which point all available lots were filled. The public market moved from Christopher Street in 1833 to the triangular area now bounded by Sixth and Greenwich Avenues and West 10th Street, where, as the Jefferson Market, it served this newly grown area which was already flourishing by the 1850's. By the mid-1800's class structure in the Village had solidified. To the north of the Square lived

the aristocracy; to the south lived the working class, comprised mostly of immigrants; and to the west was the middle class.

In 1865, one-fourth of the city's black population was concentrated in the area around Bleecker and Mac-Dougal, known as "Little Africa." The first black newspaper in the country, *Freedom Journal*, was published here in 1827, and the first black theater, the African Grove, opened two blocks east on Mercer Street in 1821. Whites were segregated into the back seats because, according to a handbill, they "do not know how to conduct themselves at entertainment for ladies and gentlemen of color." St. Benedict the Moor, the first black Roman Catholic church in the north, opened in 1833 at No. 210 Bleecker Street near Downing, where over the years a succession of immigrant churches were built.

By the 1860's, French immigrants filled the houses on Wooster, Greene, West Third and West Fourth Streest, an area then called "Frenchtown." Bars and concert halls were scattered through the neighborhood. The Black and Tan Concert Hall on Bleecker Street, also known as the "Chemise and Drawers," featured scantily clad black dancing girls who were available as prostitutes. "Scotch Ann's" was a brothel where the whores were young men with painted faces, effeminate voices, and women's names.

M any restaurants had opened in the 1840's in cozy ground-floor spaces or basements. Tucked away in the winding streets, writers, poets, actors and other intellectuals gathered and called themselves "bohemians". These thinkers sought to emulate the life many of them had enjoyed in Paris. Among them was Walt Whitman, whose favorite watering spot was Charlie Pfaff's celebrated beer cellar on Broadway near Bleecker Street. Here his followers clustered around to hear him read and speak. Among the young women who joined the Whitman admirers at Pfaff's are two famous actresses, Adah Isaacs Menken, who later became the mistress of Alexander Dumas *pere*, and Ada Clare, who enjoyed a similar relationship with the famous American composer and pianist Louis Gottschalk. They were often joined by Lola Montez, erstwhile mistress of Franz Liszt and "protegee" of King Ludwig I of Bavaria. These were avant garde women, liberated for their time.

One of the more straight-laced Villagers, Ralph Waldo Emerson, said that the raucous environment of Pfaff's was strictly for "noisy and rowdy firemen."

If Pfaff's was not the first, it was certainly among the earliest of the bohemian gathering places. Word of their existence and the unusual activities that took place in them soon spread around town. It became fashionable and adventurous for uptowners to ride to Greenwich Village for an evening of fun observing the bohemians with their strange behavior and curious dress.

But in the meantime, the tensions between North and South were considerable, even in a city as far north as New York. The new Union government did not

always make decisions that were popular.

The cause of the war was at first overwhelmingly supported by most of the people of New York City, and when a reporter from the *Illustrated London News* made a tour in June of 1861 he filed the following report: "I could easily believe myself to be in Paris or some other city devoted to military display, instead of New York, the commericial emporium of the North...here is not a house that does not display Union Colours of some kind: there is not a steeple ever so lofty that is not surmounted by a star-spangled banner; there is not a man or woman in the city that does not wear a patriotic badge of some kind. It is a mighty uprising of a united people determined to protect their flag to the last."

The war unfortunately was not over as quickly as optimists on both sides had predicted. The South seemed just as determined to succeed as the North. Both sides suffered grave losses in the ensuing months and in the early days of the war New York City lost many of its bravest sons. But on August 4, 1862, President Lincoln sent assurances to our ally in France, the Count de Gaspain, that the North was not at a loss, but "our great army has dwindled rapidly bringing the necessity for a new call earlier than was anticipated. We shall easily obtain the new levy, however. Be not alarmed," he went on to caution Gaspain, "if you shall learn that we have resorted to a draft to be part of this. It seems strange even to me, but it is true, that the Government is pressed to this by popular demand. Thousands who wish not to personally enter the service are nevertheless anxious to pay (a $600 fee) and to send substitutes, provided that they can have assurance that unwilling persons similarly situated will be compelled to do likewise."

Adjutant General Hillhouse declared on December 31, 1862 that new York State was short of its quota of volunteers by 28,517 of which, by reason of its greater concentration of population, New York City's portion was 18,523. This was a blow seemingly designed to instigate insurrection. The total population of the city was only 814,000 in 1860 and a vast majority of those citizens were poor. The war cry that had rung so clearly was suddenly hushed as many thousands of potential draftees saw that only the rich would be allowed to stay with their families. Six Hundred Dollars was a veritable fortune at a time when a entire house would rent for $147 a year, and a shack could be had for 12¢ a night!

The enrollment act was approved on March 3, 1863. A Chelsean, Colonel Robert Nugent. "Sixty-Ninth New York Volunteers, a gallant soldier, a discreet officer, an Irishman and a Democrat" was appointed assistant Provost-Marshall-General to oversee the working of the draft. The first day the drawings of the names in all wards of the city went smoothly until late in the afternoon when bloodshed broke out between the police and draftees. "Certain Ruffians" took up the cry and began to mass around the enrollment wheels. The police attempted to contain the mob but soon the militia and the National Guard were called in. Second, Third and

Although New York City had experienced riots before and would do so again, The Draft Riots of July 13-15, 1863 would never be equalled for the atrocities committed by the mob. A vast majority of the rioters were Irish, simply because most of the population of Manhattan and the gangsters and the other criminal elements of that time were Irish.

By nightfall of July 13, New York City was practically in the hands of the mob. From all quarters came reports that the small detachments of police remaining were meeting with defeat and fleeing before the rioters; and military aid was not yet available in sufficient force to accomplish anything. "Fires from a score of burning buildings pierced the darkness, and the hot stillness of the July night was made more oppressive by the columns of black smoke which hung low over the city."

Two major incidents occurred in Greenwich Village on the second day of rioting, Tuesday, July 14. According to a graphic account by Herbert Asbury, it began with two murders. "After a night of drinking and carousing in the dives and dance halls of the Bowery and Five Points, more than a thousand frenzied men and women surged into Clarkson Street before dawn and hanged William Jones, a negro, to a tree when he attempted to defend his wife and children and prevent the burning of his home. A fire was lighted beneath him and the mob danced madly about, shrieking and throwing stones and bricks at his body while it dangled above the flames. Another negro, named Williams was attacked at Washington and Leroy Streets. While half a score of rioters held him down, their leader smashed his skull with a huge stone. Women who accompanied the rioters slashed his body with knives and poured oil into the wounds, but before they could ignite the oil, they were dispersed by a detachment of police under Drill Officer Copeland and Captain John F. Dickson. This force also defeated the mob in Clarkson Street and cut down Jones's body."

These were the torments that the mob inflicted on all victims, black or white. The mob, numbering about eight thousand, later that day attempted to enter the Village up Broadway and were finally beaten back at Amity (West Third) Street.

When an uneasy peace was brought about by Government troops, at least 900 had been killed and 8,000 injured, and more than one million dollars in property had been destroyed. The corrupt city government chose not to pursue a majority of the culprits and only 19 rioters were convicted and imprisoned.

CHARGE OF THE POLICE ON THE RIOTERS AT THE "TRIBUNE" OFFICE.

SACKING A DRUG STORE IN SECOND AVENUE.

HANGING A NEGRO IN CLARKSON STREET.

Seventh Avenues the next day were a sea of maddened rioters who threw aside the police and militiamen. Negroes began to be maimed and murdered as the lusts of the mob strove to find some way to vent their anger. "The lampposts were festooned for the entire length of some streets with human carrion," one onlooker reported later after the rioters surged up across Greenwich Village via Greenwich Avenue to attack the State Arsenal at 35th Street. They were barely repulsed.

An official report tendered after the riots of July 13-15, 1863 gave this account of the fighting as the mad army swarmed across Manhattan: "The second and third day were marked by fresh outbursts and much bloodshed, bayonets and bullets were substituted for policemen's billies. The territory of the disturbance had extended to Harlem and westward beyond Sixth Avenue...when driven from one section it quickly made its appearance in another. It gradually crept over to the North (Hudson) River."

Many houses were sacked and burned. Known abolitionists and blacks were especially badly treated. The number of dead has never been known exactly, but it is believed that hundreds were killed and thousands wounded. One account gives estimated totals of more than 900 killed (of these, probably 400-500 were rioters killed by the police and military), 8,000 injured, 18 blacks hanged with five more drowned and over 70 missing. More than 50 buildings, valued at over $1,000,000 were burned (including the provost marshal's office, the Coloured Orphan Asylum, and an armory), and many others damaged.

As in other parts of the city, the Village had its share of rioting, the worst at the intersection of Grove, Christopher and West Fourth Streets. The owner of the house at No. 92 Grove is reported to have saved a number of the local blacks by hiding them from the mob. The intersection was named in 1890 for General Philip Sheridan, and there is more than a little irony that it was named for an officer in the army in a war these people died to protest.

The rioting stopped gradually as it was announced by the mayor that the draft had been suspended and the Common Council approved $250,000 towards paying the $600 enrollment fee for those poor who might have been drafted.

The draft was reinstated some time later and the city returned to the necessary task of supporting the war effort. On April 4, 1864 the city projected a magnificent Metropolitan Fair in aid of the U.S. Sanitary Commission this was the term used in those days for hospitals etc.

It was to be held on 14th Street near Sixth Avenue and offered for sale many unusual and interesting items that were donated by some citizens and purchased by others. The opening address was delivered by Joseph H. Choate and Oliver Wendell Holmes dedicated his "Army Hymn" at the celebration.

"No more its flaming emblems wave,
To bar from hope the trembling slave
No more its radiant glories shine
To blast with woe one child of Thine!"

At the end of the four day effort the Fair had raised more than a million dollars from a city that had already given so much.

The end of the war caused general jubilation but the joy was short-lived when the news of President Lincoln's assassination arrived on April 15, 1856. His body was brought by slow train from Philadelphia to New York where the cortege passed slowly up Broadway through the Village to the train that would carry him back to Washinton. "More than 60,000 soldiers and citizens formed the escort and more than a million people lined the route. Nothing before or since transpiring in the city can be compared to the universal and personal sorrow manifested by every soul of that mighty host."

The city of New York was near bankruptcy following the Civil War. Much of its monies and many of its fine young men had been sacrificed to the war effort. The city did not exist above 42nd Street in 1865, except for a few scattered villages. Railway passengers coming from the North left their trains at 27th Street and Third Avenue or at 30th Street and 11th Avenue in Chelsea. There was no comfortable way of getting from one end of the city to the other. Its architecture basically consisted of low three-and-four story houses punctuated by dozens of high church steeples. The Astor House was pointed out as a mammoth structure and a six-story building was a towering wonder.

After the Civil War the problems of transport had become almost insurmountable in the city and in the Village as well. Though the population had spread to the north, the center of business was still on the lower end of Manhattan. Traffic on the streets and avenues, particularly north and southbound, was constantly congested.

It had long been a dream to construct an elevated mode of transportation, and in 1868 the city's first elevated railway was built on Greenwich Street, called the West Side & Yonkers Patent (Elevated) Railway, it was developed by inventor Charles Harvey. By 1870 this strange structure wound its way as far north as 30th Street, and rumors spread that it would be extended the 14 miles to Yonkers. As reported in *Scientific American*, "The cars are propelled by endless wire ropes, actuated by a stationary steam engine and drum. The rope carries travelers placed at proper intervals, and rolling upon small rails. The travelers are composed of four miniature car wheels, and carry projecting studs, which, engaging with a lever arm on the car make the connection." This line was followed by construction of the Sixth Avenue elevated line in 1876, built under the direction of Dr. Rufus H. Gilbert, a former medical practitioner who had become avidly interested in transit.

Beneath the overhead trains, neighborhoods began to deteriorate. Breweries, warehouses, and small factories mushroomed. Large single family residences built in the 1820's and 30's were broken up into rooming houses. Over the years, especially between 1880 and 1890, many of the early 19th-century row houses were torn down to make way for tenements and loft buildings. The damage was severe where the waterfront west of Washington Street was filled in, extending the land to West Street. An increasing number of piers were built where ships from all parts of the world anchored.

In the ragtime era, in April of 1892, 20 men climbed to the top of the nearly completed Washington Square Arch in a typical, offbeat social gathering of the day, among them some of the Village's most influential people. Socialite Stanford White, designer of the arch, was one of those present. To the ritzy uptowners and their Village followers. "society" was of utmost importance. However, by the end of the Gay Nineties and in the early part of the 20th century, a wave of social awareness broke over New York. (White was later shot by the husband of his mistress Evelyn Nesbit at Madison Square Garden, then at 23rd Street).

The "new bohemians" considered themselves socialists, of course, and a number of them were newspaper writers who submitted stories to their papers concerning slum conditions in the city. Stephen Crane, for example, came to New York as a young reporter in 1891 and lived in various rooms on or near Washington Square. He wrote of the city poor long before his Civil War novel *The Red Badge of Courage* was to make him famous. Social work also had a strong appeal, and in 1902 Mary Simkhovich founded Greenwich House (now at No. 27 Barrow Street), patterning it after the Hull House that Jane Addams had founded in Chicago's slums. Major labor reforms were made after the disastrous Triangle Fire off Washington Square in 1911, when 146 young immigrant garment workers perished because of inadequate safety exits and the absence of elementary fire-prevention safeguards.

In the early years of the century, many of the younger gerneration leaned toward socialist views, scorning the acquisition of material wealth. They flocked to the Village, where rents were cheap and sandals and scarfs were the accepted fashion. much to their liking.

One well-known gathering place for the *literati* was the home of Mabel Dodge at No. 23 Fifth Ave. The wealthy heiress entertained not only artists and writers, but labor figures and politicians. Lively discussions seemed to be constantly in progress in her salon.

In 1910 *The Masses* began publication with Max Eastman as its editor. He and his staff worked at No. 133 MacDougal Street, the same building that housed the Liberal Club. Another publication, *Seven Arts*, began printing in 1916, and among its contributors were some of America's most famous writers—Carl Sandburg, Eugene O'Neill, Walter Lippmann, Sherwood Anderson, Robert Frost and John Dos Passos.

(Continued on page 33)

Fifth Avenue at Twelfth Street — 1895.

1876
TO
1920

AS IT WAS THEN

Fifth Avenue New York, from Start to Finish, 1911.

L ooking west down Eighth Street—the arch is barely visible at far left. Note the streetcar at middle right (The photographer has fastidiously air-brushed out the tracks and overhead cables.)

T his was the era of opulence for lower Fifth Avenue. The Vanderbilt mansions at the corner of Eighth Street have all since been demolished to allow the building of another "white elephant" in the 1960's. This photo, from a rare book of photos that detailed Fifth Avenue, block by block, was published in 1911.

O f all the buildings pictured here on lower Fifth Avenue, only the mansion on the far right remains (changed to accomodate shops at ground level). It was originally similar to the other remaining Nineteenth Century building left largely undisturbed at No. 47 Fifth Avenue (see insert). This last complete and elegant example of the type & quality of mansions that once lined this Avenue is the Salmagundi Club, whose members included John LaFarge, Louis C. Tiffany and Stanford White. It was formed in 1871 for "the promotion of social intercourse between artists." It is the oldest artist's club in the United States and painting exhibitions open to the public are sometimes held on the parlor floor, a superbly preserved interior of the period.

*T*he quiet, refined splendor of Fifth Avenue (here shown in 1911 looking north from Ninth Street) was in great contrast to the neighborhoods to the west. Here under the "Els" on Sixth Avenue and Greenwich Street, neighborhoods began to deteriorate and many of the homes from the 1820's and 30's were broken up into rooming houses. Developers began to build six-story tenements and breweries and small factories mushroomed. The Metropolitan Museum of Art and Mark Twain found homes on Fifth Avenue while the Hudson Dusters and other violent gangs grew up under the Els.

from Bank St. Looking North from an elevation

Looking North from Bank Street in 1876.

The first "El" ran along Greenwich Street from the Bowery to the rail lines in Chelsea at 31st Street. The smokestack at rear center was located at Gansevoort Street. This large brick factory effected the change in a nearby street's name from the Dutch "Great Kill" to "Great Kiln" Road, a confusion never overcome by many mapmakers. (see Section on Greenwich Village Streets).

Resembling a centerpiece on a wedding cake, The Jefferson Market Courthouse rises above the tracks of the Sixth Avenue Elevated Railway. Long a hub of commercial activity, it was erected in 1876 as a part of a complex, including a market and a jail (on the left), by Vaux and Withers who helped design Central Park.

Last used as a courthouse in 1945, this fine example of Victorian Gothic (voted the fifth most beautiful building in America in 1885) was once slated for destruction. But Villagers fomented such a public out cry that it was saved, and in 1967 the interior was expertly remodeled by Georgio Cavaglieri for use as a branch of the New York Public Library, leaving the exterior basically untouched.

In 1927, the market complex behind to the left was demolished and an awful twelve story Women's Detention Center was erected. The inmates made such a habit of catcalling to friends and/or foes on the streets below, that after nearly fifty years, community pressure forced the facility to close and the building was torn down. The site now holds an idyllic community garden famed for its roses.

This photo looking west down Tenth Street in 1902 shows many buildings that thanks to the Historic District designation have been saved, from demolition.

It is interesting to note that the building on the extreme left in the photos on this and the following page was Luke O'Connors "Columbia Gardens", better known to young people at the turn of the century as "The Working Girl's Home". John Masefield who was to become The Poet Laureate of England, worked here as a barboy—scrubbing floors and emptying spitoons.

(See pages 114-116 for additional information)

Christopher Street and Greenwich Avenue from under the Elevated, the buildings on the left were demolished when the Sixth Avenue subway was run through and those nearest the camera on the right were torn down in 1930 to construct an apartment house.

*H*udson Park was the pride and joy of Greenwich Village in the early 1900's. The horrors
of the well-publicized murders during the Civil
War in Clarkson Street on its southern side were
overcome by the stately prescence of St. Luke's
Place on the north. In the left of the above photo
you can see that magnificent Italinate row in 1894.
Note in this photo that this former graveyard (where
the Dauphin of France was rumored to be buried)
still extends straight through to Carmine Street
where Edgar Allen Poe lived in 1856. The tumult
of Seven Avenue South was still many years away.

Mayor Jimmy Walker's home on St. Lukes Place

Bocce at Hudson Park in 1958 after Hudson Park was paved over to form a playground.

Wm. Acker

A Bit of Old Greenwich Village, 7th Ave., 12th–13th Sts.   Copyright, 1905, by W. R. Morrison.

The warehouse/factory that was demolished when Seventh Avenue was put through to Varick Street.

This view taken in 1912 shows the terminus of the Avenue. The building on the previous pages would have been uptown on the right and St. Vincent's Hospital to the left. (For a clearer viewpoint see map section and page 116 for additional information [on the subway).

The photos on these two pages and on the following page illustrate the changes that occurred after Seventh Avenue South and the subways were put through. When the photo at lower left was taken of the northeast corner of Greenwich and Seventh Avenues before 1916, Seventh Avenue began its uptown drive at the intersection of Greenwich Avenue and West Eleventh Street (see photo following page). After completion of the subway tunnel, the entire western-corner block was eventually demolished and the famous Loew's Sheridan was built (seen below in 1937). In the 1970's St. Vincent's Hospital had the abandoned theatre torn down in an abortive expansion attempt. Community residents soon tired of the empty lot and established a beautiful garden similar to that which now fronts Jefferson Market. With the aid of then-Governor Cary's brother-in-law and other influential members on the board of St. Vincent's, a new hospital was built across the street and the garden was eliminated to "facilitate construction." The original hospital that had stood on the northeast corner since 1895 was demolished despite and possible to spite the considerable local opposition. Edna St. Vincent Millay gained her middle name by virtue of being born in that old building, and Dylan Thomas died there.

Opposite, top left: A rare postcard view by W.R. Morrison. This example of the popular "terraces" of the turn-of-the century was demolished when the Maritime Union built one of the ugliest buildings in New York, which is, unfortunately, still there today and is used as St. Vincent's clinic.

New-York Historical Society

Top right—Union Square looking Northwest in 1894.

Far right—S. Klein buildings (demolished)

The scenes on the left were taken by M. Cohn in 1908, when police refused to permit Socialists to hold a meeting at Union Square. A young Anarchist tried to kill some of the officers with a hand-make bomb just moments after this photo was taken. It went off in his hand. He lived and was arrested for the attempted murder of a police officer.

Police drive the crowd away from the corner of 15th Street and Union Square West after the incident (bottom left).

Please read the History segment on Union Square for further information.

Abingdon Square was a lovely, quiet residential spot in the late 1800's

The Mills House in 1896/87.

Crackling paint reveals history in 1985.

Carl Paler

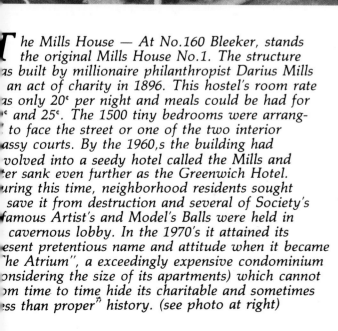

he Mills House — At No.160 Bleeker, stands the original Mills House No.1. The structure as built by millionaire philanthropist Darius Mills an act of charity in 1896. This hostel's room rate as only 20ᶜ per night and meals could be had for ᶜ and 25ᶜ. The 1500 tiny bedrooms were arrang- to face the street or one of the two interior assy courts. By the 1960,s the building had volved into a seedy hotel called the Mills and ter sank even further as the Greenwich Hotel. uring this time, neighborhood residents sought save it from destruction and several of Society's famous Artist's and Model's Balls were held in cavernous lobby. In the 1970's it attained its esent pretentious name and attitude when it became "he Atrium", a exceedingly expensive condominium onsidering the size of its apartments) which cannot om time to time hide its charitable and sometimes ss than proper" history. (see photo at right)

The avant-garde of the left in the United States and the feminist movement were more or less concentrated in Greenwich Village around this time. Various forms of Marxism were popular and Victorian morality was to be replaced by "free love".

The experience of those feminists who lived in the village during the early years of this century symbolized the "new women". Women were just beginning to leave the shelter of the home for personal careers. Feminism challenged the traditional roles that Western culture had assigned women and proclaimed their natural equality.

Most suffragists at this point, including the redoubtable Susan B, Anthony, considered the vote to be the final step for women's rights. A group of Village feminists worked to achieve a broader and more comprehensive (and thus more radical) platform of women's rights than was advocated by American suffragists in general. This group of women involved with feminism in the Village were: Crystal Eastman, Henrietta Rodman, Ida Rauh, Neith Boyce and Susan Glaspell.

All were from upper middle class families who allowed them more freedom than was given most poorer women. All used their education and the fact that they were able to support themselves (for example, two were newspaper writers, one a teacher) in the Village to the advantage of their ideological commitments. Among their male feminist sympathizers were major political activists—Max Eastman, John Reed and Floyd Dell, among others. Indeed, Idah Rauh later married Max, editor of *The Masses*.

These women were responsible for major reforms that resulted in concessions by the New York government that allowed mother with children to return to teach in public school (such mothers were banned from teaching posts prior to 1915), provided easily understood information about birth control for poor women, and cleared the way past the opposition of male bureaucrats for many later feminist reforms—all before 1920.

A wealthy patron of the arts, Gertrude Vanderbilt Whitney, established a studio in MacDougal Alley to show the works of a new generation of American artists. Among the first was a group known as "The Eight," who she encouraged in their challenge of traditionalism and for painting life "in the raw." They came from all parts of the country to the Village: Robert Henri, Everett Shinn, George Luks, William Glackens, John Sloan, Ernest Lawson, Maurice Prendergast, Arthur B. Davies. Their first show, held in 1914 in the remodeled studio on MacDougal Alley, caused an uproar. They were dubbed "The Ashcan School" for their unremitting realism and attention to the grimier details of everyday life. Four of the paintings from the show were purchased by Mrs. Whitney and formed the beginning of the Whitney Museum of American Art (which originally opened in 1931 at No. 8 West Eighth Street; the Museum is now on Madison Avenue).

Theater people flocked to the Village. A group of

Harry K. Thaw's wife tries to duck an aggressive photographer as the scandal mounts in 1906. She was the mistress of famous designer Stanford White and posed for a nude "Diana" which was mounted atop White's palatial Madison Square Garden (then on the square at Twenty-sixth Street).
An insanely jealous, Harry K. (on the right) shot Mr. White dead at an after dinner party at the Garden on June 25, 1906.

M. Cohen, 1906

Villagers, meeting while on vacation on Cape Cod, organized a group called the Provincetown Players upon their return to the city. Their first home was on Mac-Dougal Street next door to the Liberal Club, where the Washington Square Players had been organized in 1915. The two theater groups began the first experimental theater in New York; among the early members were Miriam Hopkins and Edna St. Vincent Millay; later, Bette Davis was a member of the group. Eugene O'Neill was the star playwright.

The Village was the stage upon which these young men and women of talent and genius worked and played. One group of young socially concerned writers, among them Theodore Dreiser, Upton Sinclair and Jack London, lived at No. 61 Washington Square South in a converted mansion they unabashedly called "the House of Genius." Among their favorite eating places were Polly's on MacDougal Street where Hippolyte Havel, a notorious anarchist, was cook and waiter and fond of calling the customers "bourgeois pigs." Mother Bertollotti's on West Third Street was another place where the food was cheap enough (or even free) for poor young artists.

The fervor of the young radicals was somewhat quenched by the serious years of World War I and the surge of patriotism that arose at that time. *The Masses* ceased publication, banned for supposedly inhibiting enlistments, in 1917.

After the war, progress began making ungainly strides through the Village. Seventh Avenue had been extended south through the heart of the area, and buildings had been razed without regard for historic or aesthetic value. The tunnel for the Seventh Avenue Subway was completed, and the Village became accessible to hoards of tourists. It became a mecca for sightseers and the curious, and home for the eccentric.

Antique shops by the dozens carried on their business on Greenwich Street and in the smaller side streets. Tearooms with quaint names popped up everywhere—the Mad Hatter, opened in 1916, was soon followed by the Pepper Pot, the Purple Pup, the Mousetrap and many others. Cafes also abounded and prospered, among them Puss-in-Boots, the Little Sea Maid, the Garret, and Three Steps Down. Outside they were painted brilliant blue, vermillion, blazing yellow or violent green—if not in stripes. Inside, poets read their works by candlelight and "art" was absorbed by the wide-eyed, gullible tourists.

With the advent of Prohibition in 1919, the character of the Village was dramatically changed. Restaurants and tearooms became speakeasies, particularly those on the side streets. In the eyes of some of the older Village denizens, the Village was becoming vulgarized to what Floyd Dell described as a "sideshow for tourists". Brooks Atkinson, in his memoir *East of the Hudson*, described the middle 1920's in the Village: "It was a place of free living and dissipation, of cults, bohemians and decadents, and if you regarded it through

At No. 15 Fifth Avenue stood the internationally famous Brevort Hotel, which opened in 1854, and was demolished to allow the building of another huge block-wide monstrosity of an apartment house which dares to wear the name "Brevort".
(see History Section)

The Hotel Gonfarone on MacDougal Street was one of several small hotels that sprang up around Washington Square in the 1880's. Although dwarfed by the reputation of the Brevoort, it was widely known for its hospitality and service. (MacDougal Alley is in the foreground and Eighth Street behind

*I*n 1902 Mary Kingsbury Simkhovitch founded Greenwich House in two small brick houses (at right) on Jones Street, then "the most populated street on the Lower West Side". Formed in sympathetic response to the plight of thousands of poor Italian, Irish and Middle-European-Jewish immigrants who filled the six-story-low-income tenements that had been built in the area by speculators with the collusion of the city government.

Well known locally for her significant work in Social reform, Simkhovitch's personal communication with the neighborhood eventually gained nationwide recognition. As the Village changed, Greenwich House has continually updated its programs and facilties. In addition to other duties, it was the first settlement house in the United States (1963) to treat drug abusers on an out-patient basis. Presently, in any given week about 3,000 people will pass through the doors of their present Georgian-Revival building at No. 27 Barrow Street.

Eleanor Roosevelt visits Mrs. Simkhovitch at Greenwich House in the late 1930's. Mrs. Roosevelt had an apartment at 29 Washington Square West.

Above: M. Cohen points his camera down the air-shaft of the burned-out building. At right: *The devastation was complete on the Ninth Floor. Top right: Mourners leave the improvised morgue at the 26th Street pier. Next page top: Hundreds file past the bodies hoping that their friends or family were not there.*

Below: *On the anniversary of the fire in 1985, firemen and relatives of the victims held a memorial service.*

Newsday Photo.

The Triangle Fire, 1911.

A bronze plaque at the corner of Washington Place and Greene Street discreetly marks the site of the Triangle Shirtwaist Company fire, which occured on the afternoon of Saturday, March 25, 1911. Appalling working conditions in these "sweatshops" were widely known but pressure from influential businessmen kept city and state officials from providing sufficient safety measures, until 146 lives were lost here (mainly poor Italian and Jewish women and young girls).

As a result of the investigation that followed, State laws were enacted that reformed the fire code and prohibited crowding in all commercial buildings. The owners of the Triangle were indicted, but public indignation went unheard and they were acquitted of responsibility.

saucer-eyes you could live there in a daze of constant wonder and titillation. Speakeasies and degenerate dives festered all through the vicinity...The Village was no prude; the facts of life had been gulped down whole by those who were in the trade of providing deversion for a fee...but the tolerance that protected them in their puckish minstrelries made it also possible for us to live exactly as we pleased".

In all the gaudy atmosphere and cheap flamboyance of the 20's, the Village remained a mecca for true artists. Edna St. Vincent Millay still lived in the narrowest house in the city at No. 75½ Bedford Street (also home at other times to Lionel Barrymore, and to Deems Taylor) Ruth McKenney wrote My Sister Eileen, the story of her adventurous life with her sister, while living at No. 14 Gay Street.

In 1924, Millay and others, dissatisfied with the commercialism of the Provincetown Players, founded the Cherry Lane Theater, still standing on Commerce Street, to continue work with experimental theater. In 1926, Eva LeGalliene founded the Civic Repertory Theater on 14th Street west of Seventh Avenue on the site of the old Palace Garden. Among the plays she directed there were Romeo and Juliet, Camille and Cradle Song. This was one of the first popular-priced repertory theaters and it "kept its lights"until 1933 when it gave way to the Theater Union, which produced plays with pronounced social themes.

If the Provincetown Players gave the country modern playwrights, the group that preceded it for a short while on MacDougal Street, the Washington Square Players--with Helen Westley, Phillip Moeller, Lawrence Langner and others--gave America an organization which, moving uptown as the Theater Guild, taught incredulous Broadway producers that living art could bring box-office receipts.

During the years 1910 to 1921 the area around 14th Street was at its most depressed. It was an era of burlesque houses, shooting galleries and shoddy businesses. Real estate values sank to a new low, and in 1921 many parcels of land were sold at foreclosure. S.Klein, operator of a dress establishment, bought three of these dilapidated buildings on the east side of Union Square and began a program of expansion.

While experimental theaters and protean commercial enterprises were taking over a portion of 14th Street, the Union Square area was becoming a focal point for political activities as well. Meetings and occasional clashes with the police continued with increasing frequency. On August 22, 1927, the night set for the execution in Boston of the anarchists Nicola Sacco and Bartolomeo Vanzetti, a shoemaker and a fish peddler, it was reported that "...machine guns were mounted on the roof of the six-story building (one of S.Klein's) at No.28-30 Union Square East, and were trained on a compact mass of more than five thousand tense, silent men and women, part of the angry crowd that had packed the square throughout the day. A little after mid-

night a sign was thrust outside the Daily Worker windows: 'Sacco Murdered.' Some minutes later another sign appeared: 'Vanzetti Murdered.' A throaty wail of anguish arose. A small procession that immediately formed was dispersed by the police, and several marchers were injured."

The New Masses was founded in 1926 by John Dos Passos, Edmund Wilson and Freda Kircheway in response to the social environment of the 20's, and creative artists joined the fray, manifested by such events as E.E. Cumming's 1928 play Him, the cause of violent debate between radical and conventional theater critics.

On May 18, 1929, the Communist Party led an anti-police brutality demonstration, and again the police charged. Many heads were broken and 27 of the demonstrators, including nine children, were arrested. The impact of this tragic episode upon the minds and hearts of writers and artists was undoubtedly the single most important factor in the subsequent flirtation many of them carried on with Communism.

Between World Wars I and II the Village changed very little in appearance. Except for the building of skyscraper apartment houses on Fifth Avenue and more subways--the Sixth Avenue line was cut through in the 30's--and the demolition of the Elevated, it remained a unique and undisturbed part of the city. Little Italy continued to expand its annual feasts upward toward the Village; the center of shopping was around Jefferson Market Courthouse and Eight Street.

The Great Depression which began with the stock market collapse in 1929 left artists and writers without work; the populace was hard pressed to find money for food, let alone art. But the New Deal of 1933 offered the beginning of another kind of hope. Federal aid was given for the first time to creative endeavors such as the WPA Theater and Arts Project, and this financing gave a start to many young people who later were to make significant contributions to the culture of the city—as well as to the entire country.

The musical world of the Village at this time, apart from a few well known American names such as Aaron Copeland, and later, Leonard Bernstein, was dominated by jazz. The New School for Social Research opened its controversial new building on West 12th Street in 1931, and the Little Red Schoolhouse began its pioneering role in progressive elementary education in 1932.

The end of World War II witnessed the beginning of a new building boom in the Village. In the 1940's New York University began its so-called "revitalization" program for Washington Square, acquiring all the property on the eastern and western end of Washington Square South. The new buildings erected in the 1960's had a modern, progressive look, but were generally scoffed at by architects and artists. Further, these buildings rose on sites which formerly held many landmarks and historic buildings which were lost in the "revitalization"process. Indeed, perhaps the most

Gertrude Vanderbilt Whitney, already an established sculptor, had taken a studio in MacDougal Alley in Greenwich Village. A many-sided person, at home in both the social and artistic worlds, her sympathies from the first were with the liberal artists. She was an early friend of Henri, Davies and other independents; and when the Eight held their historic exhibition at the MacBeth Gallery in New York she bought four of the seven paintings that were sold.

From 1907 on Mrs. Whitney held informal exhibitions in her studio of works by fellow artists; and in 1914 she converted the adjoining house at 8 West Eighth Street into a gallery she called the Whitney Studio, where she gave regular exhibitions of progressive and young artists. To assist her she secured the services of Juliana Force, who was to be associated with her in all her future art activities. Temperamentally these two remarkable women were entirely different...But both of them enjoyed the friendship of artists (such as the Eight) who helped to shape their policies. (from the Whitney Museum of Modern Art's 1975 Catalog-- "The Whitney Studio Club and American Art 1900-1932".

Juliana Force in her apartment above the Whitney Museum on West Eighth Street. Photograph by Cecil Beaton.

The Eight: (Top) Arthur B. Davies, William J. Glackens, Robert Henri,
Everett Shinn, (Bottom) Ernest Lawson, George Luks, Maurice Prendergast,
John Sloan. Original publicity photographs for the exhibition of the
Eight at the Macbeth Gallery, February 1908, by Gertrude Käslebier, 1907.
Courtesy of the Pennsylvania Academy of Fine Arts.

devastating destruction in the Village occured between 1950 and 1970 when historic blocks of small houses were demolished to make way for the Washington Square Village and University Village apartment complexes.

Jefferson Market Courthouse was another landmark that was almost lost in the early 1960's, but aroused Villagers waged a vigorous campaign and it was saved from the wrecker's ball. The interior was beautifully remodeled in 1967 by Giorgio Cavaglieri for use as a public library, which function it fulfills to this day.

Many times in the past politicians have tried to usurp Washington Square Park for other purposes; Boss Tweed and Tammany Hall, for example, succeeded in running Fifth Avenue, all the way through the Park down to Lower Fifth Avenue (today's LaGuardia Place) and into what is now West Broadway, although this damage was eventually undone. (The New York Tammany Society, founded in 1789, grew out of the earlier Sons of Liberty organization. Aaron Burr, was instrumental in setting up the Tammany Society politically; it was only when Tweed was in power during the 1870's, when the Tammany Society was located next to the Acadamy of Music, that Tammany Hall became a political euphemism for corruption and political bossism.)

The debates regarding the preservation of the Square have gone on continuously, but the closest battle began in the late 1930's when Robert Moses tried to put a road through the Square to Canal Street. Naturally, Villagers were outraged and the plan was withdrawn; but the untiring Moses reappeared in 1954 and produced a plan for a road to go *under* the Square. This plan was also scrapped.

In the early 1960's John F. Kennedy made his first presidential campaign speech in the Village in front of the Caffe Reggio on MacDougal Street in the same area where what were then called beatniks congregated. The beats flocked to the coffeehouses that had become political centers in the late 1940's. The beat leaders, Allen Ginsburg, Jack Kerouac, William Burroughs, Lawrence Ferlinghetti and Gregory Corso, commuted between San Francisco and the Village, but the Village was the symbol of their ideology. Mr. Corso explained that "We will not force ourselves into any hand-me-down inherited straight-jacket of cast-off moral concepts mixed with beastly superstition derived from the primitive mythology which is found in the bible".

Villagers may or may not have agreed with the beat philosophy, but they certainly did not mind adopting their long hair and bluejeans. Folk music became the standard of the time; the "Irascibles" of Abstract Expressionism had their studios in the Village as Hans Hoffman, Rothko, Pollock, deKooning, Kline, Motherwell and Brooks, among others, formed possibly the most influential American school of art. With the critical acceptance of the Circle-in-the-Square's staging in 1952 of Tennessee William's *Summer and Smoke*, off-Broadway theater began anew. Over the years it gained even more momentum, and off-off-Broadway was born on Cornelia Street where the Cafe Cino perpetuated its excesses, mother of today's Village experimental theaters producing plays with radical and even bizarre themes.

Recent years have also seen the growth of political solidarity among the gay community in the West Village. Although the gay and lesbian populace has always been prominent in the Village, it was not until the Stonewall Riots of 1969 on Sheridan Square that real strides for public—and, more important, political—acceptance began to be made. Many firsts have occurred here as this minority has gained strength. Police cooperation has grown, and both sides have united to address common problems. A Gay Senior Citizens Center has been planned for some time, and space has been found for many innovative gay service organizations. Through the efforts of a maturing gay leadership with its increasing political savvy, such gains seem certain to increase in the future.

An interesting by-product of life in the Village during the past few decades is the organization of street and block associations. First formed as a self-help measure to combat street crime, these groups of neighbors found they had much more in common than fear of criminals and went on to make their streets cleaner, to fund social programs, beautification efforts and so forth. The associations have planted trees and flowers and hold annual block parties, attended by hundreds from all over the city and from without, to raise funds for these various activities.

One of the most significant events of the last fifty years was the designation of a great portion of the Village as a Historic District in 1969. Thousands of irreplaceable structures are now protected. Unfortunately a new set of entrpreneurs have descended on the area, doubling and tripling rents for small businesss and apartments. Many historic businesses have succumbed to the pressure of this "new" greed. Absentee landlords now control more property in the Village than residents, a situation that has not existed since W.R. Grace was elected mayor by Tammany Hall in the 1880's. These corporate speculators have been encouraged to feel that they may alter or demolish with impunity by the *laissez faire* attitude of the present administration.

But Greenwich Village has weathered the storms of political and material adversity before and will, in all likelihood, remain long after present-day politicians and speculators are dead and forgotten. For ultimately it is the Villagers that make this mass of tangled streets a special place. Adamant and assembliing, demanding their right to be as they choose, loyal to their neighbors and fiercely protective of their neighborhoods, these are the men and women who will guide their domain into the Twenty-first Century.

The Metropolitan Transit Company shown here slightly before it went out of business in 1904. It was the last "horse car" to run down Broadway and cross Bleecker and Carmine to connect with Varick Street. (see street section).

Joe Coppa

AROUND WASHINGTON SQUARE

The following nostalgic look at the neighborhoods surrounding the Square just before major changes were made in the 1960's, contains much history and of course, a little gossip.

"The Music Lover"
Jack Berger, 1960.

A TOUR FROM A PARK BENCH, 1947

"Compiled under the Auspices of *The Villager*, the Community Newspaper"

The eight pleasant acres of Washington Square are the center of the literary, artistic, and intellectually liberal life that is Greenwich Village. At one time the Square kept itself aloof from the Humbler Village to the west of it. But when artists and writers re-discovered Greenwich Village just before World War I, they also moved into inexpensive studios on Washington Square South. The proper heritage of the Square, the aura of Edgar Allan Poe, Winslow Homer, Samuel F.B. Morse, and Henry James, was disrupted by a set of young iconclasts who became the idols of a new generation: John Sloan, Theodore Dreiser, John Dos Passos, Jack Reed, Willa Cather, Edna St. Vincent Millay, Eugene O'Neill.

Greenwich Village, as fervent residents define it, is a state of mind. It is a way of life, a sense of values, a corporate devotion to old houses, Cezanne, the rights of man, brick fireplaces, garlic in the salad. And so its elastic boundary easily stretched to encompass the stimulating activities in the arts which had sprung up around the Square. To the surprise of the Rhinelanders and the Stewarts, fashionable Washington Square became the heart of the Village.

Here at Washington Square the sightseeing tour actually comes to the tourist. Pick a comfortable park bench, prop up your feet, and see the Village. See the mansions of old New York and the studios of great artists. See the spot where Morse invented the telegraph, Colt the revolver, and see (with a little judicious bench-hopping) the Provincetown Playhouse, where fame found America's most distinguished playwright, Eugene O'Neill. See New York University and the famous old boarding house known as the House of Genius. See the home of the First Lady of the Village, Mrs. Franklin D. Roosevelt.

Dominating the Square is Washington Arch, which commemorates George Washington's inauguration to the Presidency. On April 30, 1889, exactly a century after the first Inauguration Day, a temporary arch was dedicated, and three years later it was replaced by the present marble structure.

William Rhinelander Steward, scion of Society and long a resident of Washington Square North, was largely responsible for erecting the arch. The designer was the most celebrated architect of the day, Stanford White. Three prominent sculptors added the ornamenta-tion: The bas relief is the work of Frederick W. Mac-Monnie, and the two statues of Washington are by Her-mon A. MacNeil (military) and A. Stirling Calder (civil).

The two other pieces of sculpture in the Square are the figure of the Italian patriot, Garibaldi, by Giovanni Turini, and a bust of Alexander Lyman Holley, the engineer who developed Bessemer steel in America, by J.Q.A.Ward.

Long before it became the address of the aristocracy and the artists, Washington Square had a fascinating history. When the Dutch bought Manhattan Island from the Indians, this patch of ground was part sandy hillocks and part swamp, left by the melting glaciers of the Ice Age.

Through the marsh that is now Washington Square from northeast to southwest, flowed turbulent little Minetta Brook. The stream leaped with trout, and in the marshes grew a profusion of berries. This was a lush bountiful land. The woods to the west (where the Village of Greenwich was built) were full of game--deer, elk, and 30-pound wild turkeys. Under the Dutch West India Company the rich land was divided into planta-tions or bouweries." From Minetta Brook to the Hudson River lay the Bossen Bouwerie, or Farm in the Woods. It soon became the finest tobacco plantation in the colony, and fattened the purse of Wouter Van Twiller, the cor-rupt governer of *Nieuw Amsterdam.*

Washington Square became city property in 1797—for a grim purpose. It was to be a Potters' Field. Under these pavements, to this day, lie the remains of thousands of persons, the paupers, the criminals,and the hastily buried victims of epidemics.

The Potters' Field was handy to the new State Prision (fore-runner of Sing Sing) which stood for 30 years at the foot of 10th. Street. Criminals from the prison were brought here to hang from the gallows which once cast its long shadow across Washington Square. Hangings were holiday events for the thrill-hunting populace. When 20 highwaymen were executed simultaneously, swinging from the limbs of a big elm tree as well as from the gallows, the spectators included no less a personage than Lafayette!

By 1823,the Potters' Field had fallen into disuse. The city converted it to "Washington Military Parade Ground," and it opened with a whopping July 4th celebration. For the picnic that followed the big bright and noisy parade,there were two oxen roasted whole, 200 hams, and beer rolled out by the barrel.

1971
Jack Berger

Romany Marie
shops the Bleecker Street Market in 1939.

Berenice Abbott

The aristocracy of New York flocked to a newly-opened Washington Square, and the one-time Potters' Field became the most fashionable address in town. The elegant houses still standing on the north side of the Square were built in the 1830's when Sailors' Snug Harbor, the charitable institution and large scale Village landlord,gave leases to the elite of New York.

Sailors' Snug Harbor was founded by Robert Richard Randall in memory of his sea-going father, Capt. Thomas Randall, Revolutionary privateer.

Robert Randall willed a stretch of land to stranded old sailors of the port of New York. He expected it to be used as a farm, a snug harbor where the old mariners could find shelter and grow their food. But by the time legal battles cleared title to the farm, it had become valuable city lots. As a result, Sailors' Snug Harbor was built on Staten Island, and the original 21 acre farm in the Village became income property which for the past 100 years and more has kept the harbor very snug indeed

The famous "Old Row" on Washington Square, built in the 1830's on Sailors Snug Harbor property, extends the full block east from Fifth Avenue. Along this line of nearly identical red brick houses have been the homes of Delanos, Stewarts, Goulds, DeForests, and Wanamakers. Across Fifth Avenue on the northwest corner is a Square brick mansion built at the same time by the William C. Rhinelanders. It is in reality three houses remodeled as an apartment, but the building preserves the dignified lines and old woodwork that made the Rhinelander House (demolished) for more than a century one of the showplaces of the square.

Both Rhinelander House and the "Old Row" are considered fine examples of Greek Revival architecture, the prevalent style when the Village had it first boom. Architects especially admire the doorways, which retain graceful Georgian lines, set behind Greek columns. The similarity of houses in the Old Row is not an accident. They were built according to a master plan, at the instigation of John Johnston, who in 1831 built the first house at number 7. Mr. Johnston's was one of the founders of New York University. Through more than a century, the house was occupied by four generations of his family.

The corner house in the Old Row was built by Mr. Johnston's business partner. Later it was the home of the city's Mayor Edward Cooper, son of the great engineer and inventor, Peter Cooper. Eugene Delano, a relative of President Roosevelt, lived here until his death in 1919, when the place was bought by Rodman Wanamaker.

Another noteworthy house is number 8, once the official residence of New York's mayors. It became the home of three, including George B. McClellan, son of the Civil War general who ran for President against Lincoln. Number 6, where stone lions flank the stoop, was the town house of Lispenard Stewart. Scion of one of the reigning Society families, he was called the Beau

Brummel of Washington Square, and considered the most eligible bachelor of the late Mrs. Astor's balls.

Sailors' Snug Harbor has in recent years remodeled most of the Row--behind their aristocratic front--into modern apartments. One of their recent tenants was Rose Franken, who lived here when she scored a triple hit with "Claudia," as best-selling novel, play, and movie.

Originally the whole block of houses wore the same haughty facade, but now No. 3 near the end is out of line and out of symmetry. Of all the Old Row, nevertheless, this ugly duck has the most enduring claim to celebrity. John Dos Passos lived for five years in the rear studio and wrote "Manhattan Transfer." Rockwell Kent, the famed graphic artist, had a studio here. So had painter Ernest Lawson. Among current residents are the artist and critic, Walter Pach, and Edward Hopper, whose whitewashed studio on the top floor has turned out such distinguished paintings as the Metropolitan's "Tables for Ladies" and "Williamsburg Bridge."

New York University occupies the whole East side of Washington Square and a block of buildings beyond it. N.Y.U. is not a state university. It is a privately endowed institution, founded in 1831 for the revolutionary purpose of teaching practical subjects as well as the classics. The founder was Thomas Jeffereson's Secretary of the Treasury Albert Gallatin.

A serious riot which has gone down in the history of organized labor marked the construction of N.Y.U.'s first building. The contractor planned to save expenses by using stone cut by the convicts of Sing Sing, but the Stonecutter's Guild protested with the first labor demonstration ever staged in New York. The National Guard was called out, and for four days Washington Square was an armed camp.

The old Gothic tower, which was replaced in 1894 by the present, blockwide Main Building, was the place where Samuel Morse invented the telegraph, and Colt developed the revolver. Professor Morse was a young art instructor who had a hobby--tinkering with electrical inventions. One day in 1838 he amazed his students and the world by clicking out the first telegraph message ever sent as a public demonstration. The message which flashed from one N.Y.U. classroom to another began, " Attention, the Universe..."

Modern photography also stems from the early N.Y.U. faculty. In 1840, John William Draper of the Science Department was experimenting with the daguerreotype process. He took his sister Catherine up to the roof of the school building and snapped the first picture of a human face by sunlight.

Samuel Colt was not a faculty member, but a lodger in the Gothic tower. He lived in one of the classrooms which the struggling University rented in order to eke out it professors' salaries. Using a model whittle from wood, Colt developed his first revolver, and fired a shot still heard around the world.

N.Y.U. can also claim. as one--time tenants three

Artists in
Macdougal Alley, 1968.
Wm. Acker

An Opening of the Whitney Museum on
Eighth Street in 1936.

Berenice Abbott

of the real giants of American arts and letters. They were Walt Whitman, poet of Democracy, whose free verse shocked a generation and pointed the way for modern poetry; Brander Mattews, eminent man of the theatre; and Winslow Homer, the powerful painter of the Sea, who was at the time he moved here just a magazine artist studying painting in night school. During the period when he lived on the Square Homer was sent to make spot news drawings of Abraham Lincoln's inauguration and the Civil War battle fields. He returned to paint his great "Prisoners from the Front," now in the Metropolitan.

Before N.Y.U. overspread the blocks to the south and east, the showplace of this elegant neighborhood was the home of Cornelius Vanderbilt. Although he could buy and sell railroads and steamship companies, the big, rough, hard-swearing, self-made magnate was snubbed by Society. In 1846 he put up the fanciest town house on Washington Place and surrounded it with the most elaborate gardens. When his wife persistently refused to join him in crashing Washington Square Society, he clapped the lady into a sanitarium for the insane until she came to her senses. Vanderbilt always won out. In the end, even his new neighbors learned to call him "Commodore."

Novelist Henry James and his elder brother, William, the outstanding American psychologist and philosopher of the last century, spent most of their childhood in the Village. Henry James was born April 15, 1843, at 5 Washington Place, in a house that stood at the corner of Mercer Street, two blocks east of the Square. After a sojourn in Europe the family of scholars came back to the Village, first to 11 Fifth Avenue, and then to a mansion at 57 West 14th Street, near Avenue of Americas. The famous brothers grew up attending a succession of local private schools, and playing in Washington Square park.

Henry James preferred to live abroad in a more rarified cultural atmosphere, but the novelist returned to write one of his best known books, "Washington Square." In it he gave the often-quoted characterization of the section: "It has a kind of established repose which is not of frequent occurence in other quarters of the long, shrill city; it has a riper, richer, more honorable look...the look of having had something of a history."

The rosy brick structure on Washington Square East, now marked Students' Building, was once an exclusive bachelors' residence, The Benedick. Among the literary elite who once lived here were Robert Chambers, author of "The King In Yellow," Hutchens Hapgood, and Gelett Burgees, humorist who lived to regret that he had "never seen a purple cow." Here Burgess wrote and drew his first book of 'Goops."

(All of the following buildings along Washington Square South have since been demolished by N.Y.U. -ED

The dilapidated corner house (on Thompson Street,) clinging to its neighbor like a barnacle, may have been here when the Square was still Potters Field. In any case, it is considered the oldest building on the Square. Nearby at 69 Washington Square South is Our Lady Of Mercy chapel and school. Conducted by the Marianites of Holy Cross, a French order of Catholic Sisters, it goes back to 1888, when this section of New York was the *Quartier Latin.*

Big names in American art are linked with the somewhat battered brick houses along the next block, as well as with studios the length of the Square. It would be possible to write a history of painting and sculpture in America, mentioning only artists who have been associated with Greenwich Village. In such a history, the focus would fall on the artists of Washington Square.

William Glackens and Ernest Lawson had a studio, a generation ago, in the red brick corner house, number 64. They were two of The Eight who rebelled against sugary painting at the National Academy and staged their own exhibition--now recognized as the birth of modern art in America. Five of the famous Eight have lived around the Square. (The others are John Sloan, Maurice Prendergast, and Everett Shinn, who had his studio on Washington Square North) Glackens never deserted the Village. He lived and painted for 20 years in his home at 10 West Ninth Street, where every fall Mrs. Glackens held a memorial exhibition of his work.

Alexander Brook, whose elegant portraits of Hollywood stars have lately given this important painter a wide public, lived at 62 Washington Square South until his move to Savannah. Perhaps equally well known is the painter who shared his studio--his former wife, Peggy Bacon. Miss Bacon lived on East 13th Street.

"The House of Genius" is a title the crowing years have conferred on 61 Washington Square South. For a half century it was a boarding house, a fabulous establishment run by Mme. Marie Branchard, which attracted a relay of young writers and artists who have since won fame. Adelina Patti was one of the first boarders, and the brilliant star of the opera once rehearsed her entire company of "Cavalleria Rusticana" in the parlor.

Theodore Dreiser came to the boarding house in 1915, so discouraged with his journalistic failures that he decided to give up writing altogether. Ten years later he wrote the first monumental piece of realism in this country's literature, "An American Tragedy." With Dreiser was his brother Paul Dresser, the musician who composed the popular song for which Theodore supplied the words, "Oh, the moonlight's fair tonight along the Wabash...From the fields there comes the breath of new-mown hay..."

O. Henry lived here for a short time with his daughter, Margaret, who married another boarder, artist Oscar Cesare. Stephen Crane worked on his classic, "The Red Badge of Courage," while he lived at Madame's.

"Television Man"
Flo Fox, 1979.

Famous painter John Sloan is pictured here in his Village studio in the late 1930's after many years as leader of the art world. As leader of the "Ashcan School" of art he was notorious for outrageous outings on the top of Washington Square Arch (there's a stairway inside).

Berenice Abbott

Frank Norris, author of "The Pit" and "The Oct-
opus," was one of the geniuses of the boarding house.
Another was Will Irwin, the Saturday Evening Post
writer, who live in number 60. He and his wife, novelist
and feminist leader Inez Haynes Irwin, owned a home
on W. 11th Street.

Alan Seeger, author of one of the great war
poems, "I Have a Rendezvous with Death," lived here in
1912 before he went overseas to keep that rendezvous.
After his death a tree was planted in the park just opposite the House of Genius, as his memorial.

Genius has lodged in rooming houses hereabouts
for more than a hundred years. Edgar Allan Poe and his
family lived in one during the winter of 1845-46, the
year that was to be the crest of his brilliant and tragic
life. The place still stands, at 85 West Third Street, a
block southward down Thompson Street and around the
corner to the right. Although it has been refurbished
beyond recognition for the present tenant (N.Y.U.fraterni-
ty house) it is the same building in which Poe lived
when he published "The Raven," and became, almost
overnight, the famous poet in America. He had put the
finishing touches on the poem the preceding year, while
he was living near-by (in a boarding house which then
stood at 15 West Third Street) and had read it to the
admiring salon of Anne Lynch, at 116 Waverly Place.
Publication of "The Raven" was so momentous an event
that it promptly established New York, rather than rival
Boston or Philadelphia, as the country's literary capital!

Poe was a familiar figure on Washington Square-
not the mad poet, but a handsome, gracious, witty
Southern gentleman. He was acclaimed besides as a
brilliant critic, editor, and author of chilling short
stories, "The Gold Bug,""The Fall of the House of
Usher,""Murders in the Rue Morgue." In the last he had
developed the technique of today's murder mysteries.

In the vacant corner lot at Thompson Street once
stood a ramshackle building originally built as the
hangman's house, when a gallows stood on Washington
Square. During the Bohemian era the place became
Bruno's Garret, sided over by the professional Bohemian, Guido Bruno. In Bruno's numerous small books
and periodicals appeared the early works of some of today's well-known writers. His backer was a famous son
of a famous Villager--Charles Edison, who was manager
of an Edison phonograph store, up Fifth Avenue.

*William Acker took these photos of MacDougal
Street in the early 1960's. The Jumble Shop (near
MacDougal Alley) was the area's intellectual tea
room in the madcap days following World War I
and a speakeasy during Prohibition. When pictured
here, it was the hangout of some of the more well-
heeled "Beatniks".*
*Allen Ginsburg read his poems at the
Gaslight Cafe, the first of many coffee houses to
offer offbeat poetry and music for the "Beat Generation".*

Across Thompson Street stands Judson Memorial Baptist Church. The flat red brick facade just behind it is Judson Health Center, founded in 1921 by Dr. Eleanor A. Campbell, who was its director. The Center conducts clinics, and especially promotes health education and preventive medicine.

Since Judson Memorial church opened in 1891, its familiar square tower and cross have been a landmark to Villagers. The church is a monument to Rev. Adoniram Judson, the first missionary to any faith to go from America to a foreign land. In the cornerstone of this church lies the first copy of the Bible of Burmese, translated by the missionary.

The memorial church was erected by Rev. Judson's som, Dr. Edward Judson, who became it first pastor. Stanford White was the architect, and sculptor adorning the baptismal pool is by Herbert Adams. The windows are the work of John LaFarge, the great painter who revived the lost art of stained glass making in America.

The Judson's church tower doubles as a college dormitory. The belfry is part of the adjoining building, now owned by N.Y.U. but originally opened as the Judson hotel, by two associates of Dr. Judson, Mr. and Mrs. James Knott. It was the small beginning of one of New York's great chains, the Knott Hotels.

Three famous poets, in their salad days, shared a studio at the Judson: William Vaughn Moody, Ridgely Torrence, and Edwin Arlington Robinson. Another resident was arctic explorer Vilhjalmur Stefansson, who was a prominent figure in the Village.

John Sloan, one of the Eight subversive fathers of modern art in America, lived for nine years in the studio of the adjoining building, now the Judson Annex of N.Y.U. The studio had originally been built by George Inness, Jr., son of the great painter of Hudson River landscapes. John Sloan preferred to paint Greenwich Village backyards, alley cats, and the Sixth Avenue"EL." Because of his fondness for back-street subjects, critics nicknamed the Eight "The Ash Can School" and "The Black Gang." Examples of Sloan's ashcan art are now at home in the Metropolitan--one of them the fine portrait of a favorite Village rendezvous, The "Hotel Lafayette," which he painted in this studio.

Maurice Prendergast, the Impressionist among the famous Eight, lived and painted for 10 years at 50 Washington Square South.

The studios of the next block (Sullivan to MacDougal now demolished) are old buildings owned by Columbia University, wearing new faces added by one of the Village's best known landlords, Papa Stunsky. The property includes houses on Third Street, remodeled so that they are hind-side-before, their front doors opening into the back yard garden of the Washington Square houses. The central garden, surrounded by steep-roofed studios, and crossed by flagstone walks, might be a courtyard in Paris.

The rosy brick building with French windows

(number 42) was another of the famed Washington Square rooming houses. Here, for a short time between muck-raking expeditions, lived Lincoln Steffens, the great journalist.

Steffens came to the square with Jack Reed, the poet and political firebrand who lies buried with a hero's honors beside the Kremlin wall in Moscow. When he lived here (in the third floor back, with three Harvard classmates) Reed wrote a little book in verse, "The Day in Bohemia," picturing a carefree life with Steffans, Walter Lippman, Will Irwin, Harry Kemp, and Alan Seeger. A more serious Jack Reed later wrote a ringing history of the Russian revolution, "Ten Days That Shook the World," in about 10 days and night of feverish work, in a hide-away he rented for the purpose near Sheridan Square. (in reality he wrote in Patchin Place - ed.)

Louise Bryant, Reed's abeautiful and brilliant wife, was with him on Washinton Square and followed him to Russia on his ill starred mission for the left-wing Socialists. At the State funeral with which Russia buried him she met her next husband—William C. Bullitt, later ambassador to France.

Look with respect at the first building below the corner on MacDougal Street. The brash new front of the Provincetown Playhouse marks the most important spot in the history of the American theatre. Here in a hall that had been a bottling works the brilliant experimental troupe of Provincetown Players presented works that were to revolutionize the theatre—including Eugene O'Neill's first great plays. In another of the buildings now united behind the new brick front, the august Theatre Guild also had its beginnings.

The cradle of experiental theatre on Washington Square was the old Liberal Club. (The Salle des Champagnes, a plush wine cellar and Village art gallery popular with N.Y.U. students, occupies the building once sacred to the Liberals.) The club attracted all intellectual rebels—poets Louis Untermeyer and Vachel Lindsay; author Sherwood Anderson; The Masses editors, Max Eastman and Floyd Dell; and several Villagers, including Robert Edmond Jones, Helen Westley, and Lawrence Langner, who had subersive ideas about the plays on Broadway. One Spring evening in 1915 a group of them were discussing the theatre in Boni's Washington Square Bookshop, which adjoined the Liberal Club. On the spot they formed the Washington Square Players and cast their first play. The enterprise burgeoned into the Theatre Guild, now the most important producer on Broadway. Lawrence Langer, was director of the Guild, and its radio and motion picture subsidiaries. He and his wife (actress Armina Marshall) were also co-authors of the hit plays, "The Pursuit of Happiness" and "Suzanna and the Elders."

After the Washington Square Players came a group that had stage some interrestin one-act plays on a wharf at Provincetown, the summer village at the tip of Cape Cod, and they gave the theatre its name. George

Cram Cook was their life spirit. With him was his wife, Susan Glaspell, who wrote for the troupe "The Inheritors," the play that gave the first role to a beautiful young actress named Ann Harding. Miriam Hopkins also got her start at the Provincetown, and in one of the last seasons, under director James Light, a small part went to Bette Davis of E. Eighth Street. Another aspiring actress was a redhaired Irish girl who found fame instead as a poetess, Edna St. Vincent Millay.

The genius of the Provincetown Players was Eugene O'Neill, a slim young man with great melancholy eyes, less sure of his won power than was director "Jig" Cook. He had a sheaf of wonderful, rebellious, vital plays. One after another Cook staged them, in this cramped, barren theatre—"Bound East for Cardif," "Ile," "The Long Voyage Home," "The Hairy Ape," "Emperor Jones." The startling plays had startling settings by Cleon Throckmorton, whose stage design studio was on W. Third Street, and by Robert Edmond Jones, who worked with O'Neill in "The Iceman Cometh."

One-act plays that are the meat of every drama class came out of the Provincetown: Susan Glaspell's "Trifles," and (with Jig Cook) "Suppressed Desired." "Lima Beans", by the poet and anthologist Alfred Kreymborg (a Villager now living on Charles St.); plays by Edna St. Vincent Millay, Harry Kemp, John Reed, Maxwell Bodenheim, Lawrence Langnor.

Back in the hoop-skirt era, 137 MacDougal Street was for 17 years the home of Nathaniel Currier, founder of the firm of popular print-makers, Currier and Ives.

Washington Square West has been overwhelmed by the 20th Century.

The Hotel Holley, 32 Washington Square W., has in its lobby the only known monument erected to a brook. The pretty fountain honors Minetta Brook—the turbulent stream that once crossed Washingotn Square—and incidentally it perpetuates the Village's favorite legend. Romantic residents insist that the little brook refused to die when the city swept it away, but found a subterranean cavern where it babbles yet. Hardened scientists say it isn't so, but the Village prefers to keep its legend.

The handsome tapestry brick apartment at the north corner of the Square (number 29) is the home of Mrs. Fanklin D. Roosevelt.

A large apartment on one of the upper floors was to have been the New York residence of the late President and Mrs. Roosevelt when he retired. The President liked his Village apartment, enjoyed the outlook over the trees in the square, and the splendid view of the Hudson river from the dining room window. Mrs. Roosevelt now lives here much of the time. and the neighbors often meet her takin a turn along the Square with her dog, the President's black Scottie, Fala.

(excerpted from *The Villager*, 1947)

WINTER 1909

Villager Florence Smith,
Actress and Model, as she appeared in
The Burr Macintosh Monthly.

WINTER 1888

Still heralded as the worst snowstorm in recent
momory, the Blizzard of '88 shows its enormity
in these rare photos. Snow has already started to pile high
near the Presbyterian Church on Fifth Avenue (top left).
It is still falling (top right) as workers try to
clear Waverly Place alongside the old N.Y.U. main
building (demolished 1894) and drifts that were sometimes
as high as first-story windows have finally been cleared
in West Twelfth Street near Sixth Avenue (right).

1912

Bitter cold hampered firemen's efforts during the spectacular fire that took six lives at the Equitable Life Insurance Company at Jones Street and Broadway on January 9, 1912

Joe Coppa.

Come to St. Joseph's Annual CHRISTMAS FAIR!
Casserly Hall, 371 Sixth Avenue from 9:00 A.M. until 5:00 P.M.
Fun for everyone - Games, Refreshments, Gifts and Baked Goodies too!

WINTER NOW

The photo on the right shows the beauteous Judson Memorial Church and the strange "modern" chapel erected by New York University.

Susan Maytell.

The wonderful lighted tree under the arch attracts carolers on Christmas.

"After college and the war(WWI) most of us drifted to Manhattan, to the crooked streets south of Fourteenth... We came to the Village without any intention of becoming Villagers. We came because living was cheap, because friends of ours had come already (and written us letters full of enchantment), because it seemed that New York was the only city where a young writer could be published. There were some who stayed in Europe after the war and others who carried their college diplomas straight to Paris: they had money. But the rest of us belonged to the proletariat of the arts and we lived in Greenwich Village where everyone else was poor.

There were two schools among us: those who painted the floors black (they were the last of the aesthetes) and those who did not paint the floors... The streets outside were those of Glenn Coleman's early paintings: low-red-brick early nineteenth-century houses, crazy doorways, sidewalks covered black snow and, in the foreground, an old woman bending under a sack of rags.....It didn't matter that we were penniless: we danced to old squeaky victrola records - You called me Baby Doll a year ago; Hello, Central, give me No man's Land - we had our first love affairs, we stopped in the midst of arguments to laugh at jokes as broad and pointless as the ocean, we were continually drunk with high spirits....As we walked down Greenwich Avenue we stopped to enjoy the smell of hot bread outside of Cushman's Bakery (at Tenth Street)

You woke at ten o'clock between soiled sheets in a borrowed apartment; the sun dripped over the edges of the green window shade. On the dresser was a half-dollar borrowed the night before... even at wartime prices it was enough to buy breakfast for two-eggs, butter, a loaf of bread, a grapefruit...Dinner provided itself, and there was always a program for the evening. On Fridays there were dances in Webster Hall(near Washington Square) attended by terrible uptown people who came to watch the Villagers at their revels and buy them drinks in return for being insulted; and on Saturdays everybody gathered at Luke O'Connors saloon, the Working Girl's Home....

-Malcolm Crowley in Exiles Return

Wm. Acker.

The bust of Alexander L. Holley guards a deserted park.

He was the technical writer, engineer, metallurgist and industrialist who introduced the manufacture of Bessemer steel to the United States. Holley died in 1882 and this monument was erected in 1890.

William Acker

SPRING brings artists by the score to Washington Square.

Cool calmness of Spring brings couples to the feet
of Garibaldi; tradition has it that the statue will
turn his head to follow a virtuous woman.

Guiseppe Garibaldi (1807-1882) . Erected in 1888 by
the Italian Community of New York for one of the
greatest guerrilla generals in history. His conquest of
Sicily and Naples in 1860 led to the unification of
Italy under the Royal House of Savoy. (by Giovanni Turini)

G. Dahlberg

THE HUDSON DUSTERS

The Hudson Dusters controlled the West Side of Manhattan below thirteenth street and eastward to Broadway, the western frontier of Paul Kely's kingdom, although their right to the later thoroughfare was bitterly contested by a small gang called the Fashion Plates. They also ranged as far south as the Battery, but their principal theater of operations was the Greenwich Village district, where a maze of crooked, winding streets offered excellent hiding places. There they had displaced the Potashes, the Boodle Gang, and other combinations of the early nineties. The Dusters were friends and allies of the Gophers, many of their leaders having formerly been members of the Hell's Kitchen gang who had moved southward when the Kitchen became too hot to hold them, but they held aloof from the feuds of the Eastmans, the Five Pointers, and other gangs of the East Side. Their principal enemies were the Marginals and the Pearl Buttons, who disputed with them for the privilege of plundering the docks and shipping along the Hudson River water front. In later years, after the Hudson Dusters had been smashed by the police and their captains had succumbed to the drug habit or had been sent to Sing Sing for various crimes, the Marginals, under the leadership of Tanner Smith, became the dominant gang of the district, subduing the Pearl Buttons and reducing them to the status of vassals.

The Hudson Dusters were organized in the late nineties by Kid Yorke, Circular Jack, and Goo Goo Knox, who had fled the Gopher domain after leading an abortive insurrection against the reigning prince. Later leaders of unusual notoriety and prowess were Red Farrell, Rickey Harrison, Mike Costello, Rubber Shaw, and Honey Steward, while King Kong became known as the most accomplished thief of the gang. Ding Dong prowled the streets attended by half a dozen young ragamuffins, who clambered onto express wagons and threw off packages to their master. Ding Dong clutched them to his bosom and fled into the crooked streets of Greenwich Village, while the driver of the wagon and the police bent themselves to the hopeless task of catching the boys. When the gang was founded headquarters were established in a building at Hudson and Thirteenth streets, the owner of which, under compulsion, donated two rooms for a club house. As the gang increased in numbers and power these quarters became too small, and the Dusters came into possession of an old house in Hudson street below Horatio, later the site of the Open Door Mission. There they installed a piano, and at all hours of the night danced and caroused with the prostitutes of the water front, becoming a nuisance and an affliction unto the honest householders and merchants of the neighborhood, upon whom they livied for supplies. But few complains were made, for the Dusters were quick to revenge slights or betrayals whether fancied or real. Once when a saloon keeper scornfully refused to provide half a dozen kegs of beer for a party, the Dusters invaded his establishment, wrecked the fixtures, and carried away his entire stock of liquors. But the police eventually took cognizance of the situation and made several raids upon the Hudson street house, at length smashing the piano and throwing the furnishings into the street. The Dusters moved into Bethune Street, and thence to various points as the Strong Arm Squad searched them out.

The journalists were very fond of the Hudson Dusters, and their activities were much described, so that they became one of the best known gangs of the period. And while they were never such fighters as the Eastmans, the Fire Pointers, and the Gophers, they were a rare collection of thugs and much of their reputation was deserved. Perhaps ninety per cent of the Dusters were cocaine addicts, and when under the infuluence of the drug were very dangerous, for they were insensible to ordinary punishment, and were possesed of great, if artificial bravery and ferocity. They seldom attacked the police in force, but whenever they had a grievance against an individual officer it was well for him to request a transfer, for sooner or later he was assaulted and maimed. Such a catastrophe happened to Patrolman Dennis Sullivan of the Charles street station, who announced during the last years of the Dusters' power that he intended, single-handed, to smash the gang. He succeeded in arresting ten of the gangsters, including Red Farrell, the leader, and his ambitions were discussed at great length at various meetings of the Dusters in Hudson and Bethune streets. It was finally decided that Sullivan must be taught a lesson, and the decision was approved by a Greenwich Village politician who utilized the Dusters at election time as repeaters and sluggers, and who felt that an attack upon the policeman would prove to the political higher-ups that the Hudson Dusters really controlled their territory. So one night in Greenwich street, as Patrolman Sullivan was about to arrest a member of the gang against whom a tradesman had complained, the Dusters pounced upon him when his back was turned, and he went down fighting valiantly against a score of slugging, kicking thugs. His coat was stripped from his back, his nightstick, shield and revolver taken away, and he was badly beaten with stones and blackjacks. When he had been knocked unconscious the Dusters withdrew, but determined to give him a permanent injury. He was therefore rolled over on his back, and four of the gangsters stepped forward and ground their heels in his face, inflicting frightful wounds. Police reserves took him to a hospital, where he remained for many weeks.

The successful attack upon Patrolman Sullivan aroused a sensation throughout gang circles, and the Gophers formally congratulated the Hudson Dusters upon the thoroughness of the job, and especially upon the added touch of stamping. One Lung Curran, who finally succumbed to the affliction which had given him his sobriquet, was in the tuberculosis ward of Bellevue Hospital when he heard the news, and celebrated the exploit in poetry, for he had long been the acknowledged bard of the West Side gangsters:

> Says Dinny, "Here's me only chance
> To gain meself a name;
> I'll clean up the Hudson Dusters,
> And reach the hall of fame."
> And his shield they took away,
> It was then that he remembered
> Every dog has got his day.

from the *Gangs of New York*, 1939

Many of the Hudson Dusters were wiped out in a shootout with police near their 13th Street "home" just before the beginning of WW I. Some of the remainder fled to Hell's Kitchen to join the embryonic Westies Gang.

The Peculiar Pub would probably have shocked Mrs. James Fenimore Cooper when she returned from France in 1833.
Samuel F. B. Morse helped the Coopers select this Federal style residence on Bleecker Street's exclusive Depau Row, which Mrs. Cooper later described as "too magnificent for our simple French tastes."

And of course some of the former customers of Marta's wanted to shock the populance in the 1920's. Elinor Wylie met several admirers here (including William Rose Benet and John Dos Passos) while she was poetry editor for Vanity Fair.

Carl Paler

G. Dahlberg

THE CURIOUS OBELISK

*S*omewhere between May 24 and July 12, 1762, a statue of British General James Wolfe, Hero of Quebec, was put into position (at approximately Fourteenth Street and Eighth Avenue). It was the first such memorial in New York, except familiar George III in Bowling Green. For years when a fashionable Manhattan youth wished a country drive with the girl of his fancy, he would proceed (in good weather) out the Greenwich Road (practically our Greenwich Street) which then ran along the river's edge; after a rainstorm, and during the period of high tides, the causeway across Lispenard's salt meadows was apt to be under water, so by 1768 a lane was opened westward from the Bowery Road, through Art Street (Astor Place) and "through the Sand Hill" to a bridge over Minetta Brook and the long straight road (Monument Lane) direct to the Wolfe memorial. The road of access to the bridge was our present slanting Greenwich Avenue. It was slanting because the bridge was naturally at right angles to the brook, and the lane continued in the same line. Which explains why so many Village streets are askew with those east of Sixth Avenue.

In especially agreeable company the driver on this pleasure jaunt would continue north along the Southampton Road to where it became Love Lane (Abingdon Road, the present Twenty-first Street); should his enthusiasm mount, it was really not far behind a spanking trotter, east and northeasst, to the Kissing Bridge (Third Avenue at Seventy-seventh Street) then a sufficiently remote spot to give uninterrupted scope for the traditional observance. And if he found himself inspired, after the fourmile trip back down the Eastern Road and the Bowery, to make use then of the older Kissing Bridge in Chatham Street (Park Row) across Old Wreck Brook and marking the city's limits at the time of the Revolution, and the primitive Love Lane on the near-by Rutgers estate—it would be fairly certain that he agreed with Reverend Mr. Burnaby, the visiting English Divine, who found this osculatory custom "curious, yet not displeasing."

So the monument, while perhaps not a complete end in itself, was a familiar object to thousands of people during the seven or eight years it stood there. Besides, a newspaper advertisement of 1762 announced as just brought to town a "most curious Piece of Work, representing a Country Seat, with the Chapel, Summer House, Flower Garden and Grottoes belonging to it; also a Monument in Memory of General Wolfe, on the Top of which is the Image of Fame, below which are the Enseigns bearing the English Standards; in the Body of the Piece is the Corps on a Couch, at the Foot of which is Minerva Weeping, at the Head is Mars, pointing to General Amherst, who stands at a small Distance, as meaning, Behold a Living Hero, with other Pieces too tedious to mention...the whole is inclosed in a Glass Case."

The ultimate mystery remains: What became of this elaborate and cumbersome "Piece"? It was there at the end of the road, Minerva still weeping, when Ratzen surveyed for his noted plan in 1766-1767. Yet when Gerard Bancker mapped the city in 1773, it was gone. To this day that is all we know. Lost, strayed, or stolen 170-odd years ago: one formidable monument, loaded to the gunwales with symbolism, and weighing many tons.

Lanier, *Greenwich Village, Yesterday and Today*—1949.

Clyde Romero created an obelisk of his own at the southern edge of Washington Square Park from the stump of a topped dead tree. Mr. Romero describes wood sculpting thusly: "When you hit it, the tool bites into the wood—you feel a sensation through your entire body— like when you strike a nail, if it goes in, it feels good." The piece is called "An Erection to Hannibal."

Carl Paler

STONEWALL LIBERATION DAY PARADE

LATE IN THE EVENING of Friday, June 27, 1969, deputy inspector Seymour Pine and seven other officers from the Public Morals Section of the First Division of the New York City Police Department set out to close the Stonewall Inn, a gay bar near the corner of Christopher Street and Seventh Avenue in Greenwich Village, just across from Sheridan Square. Arriving shortly after midnight, the police presented the Stonewall's manager with a warrant charging that liquor was being sold without a license, announced that employees would be arrested, and stood at the door to check patrons as they were ushered out one by one. Following routine practice, the authorities released customers who could produce identification and asked those who could not, plus suspected cross dressers, to step aside to be taken to the station for questioning.

Partly because the extreme unconventionality of their lives gave them little status and security to lose, most of those dismissed from the Stonewall chose not to run to safety but to gather across the street to wait for their friends. In the words of reporter Lucian Truscott IV, who had come to watch from the offices of the Village Voice just fify yards away:

Suddenly the paddywagon arrived and the mood of the crowd changed. Three of the more blatant queens—in full drag—were loaded inside, along with the bartender and doorman, to a chorus of catcalls and boos from the crowd. A cry went up to push the paddywagon over, but it drove away before anything could happen. With its exit, the action waned momentarily. The next person to come out was a lesbian, and she put up a struggle—from car to door to car again. It was at that moment that the scene became explosive. Limp wrists were forgotten. Beer cans and bottles were heaved at the windows, and a rain of coins descended on the cops. At the height of the action, a bearded figure was plucked from the crowd and dragged inside...

Three cops were necessary to get [him] away from the crowd and into the Stonewall. The exit left no cops on the street, and almost by signal the crowd erupted into cobblestone and bottle heaving. I heard several cries of "Let's get some gas," but the blaze of flame which soon appeared in the window of the Stonewall was still a shock. As the wood barrier behind the glass was beaten open, the cops inside turned a fire hose on the crowd.

Truscott's story, published the following Wednesday on the front page of the Village Voice, was the source of what most people learned about the rioting on Christopher Street. An eyewitness account by one of the rioters for the underground paper Rat offered a somewhat different perspective:

The crowd grew larger and more agitated as the squad car drove off and a wagon pulled up. People began beating the wagon, booing, trying to see who was being hauled out and off. Several pigs were on guard and periodically threatened the crowd unless they moved back. Impossible to do.

A couple more were thrown into the van. We joined in with some who wanted to storm the van, free those inside, then turn over the van. But nobody was yet prepared for theat kind of action. Then a scuffle at the door. One guy refused to be put into the van. 4 or 6 cops guarding the van tried to subdue him with little success...

Several other tried rescuing the guy held by the cops, but the latter escaped into the Stonewall. Soon the van pulled out leaving the street unguarded. A few pigs outside had to flee for their lives inside and barricade themselves in. It was too good to be true. The crowd took the offensive. The cat in the tee-shirt began by hurling a container of something at the door. Then a can or stone cracked a window. Soon pandemonium broke loose. Can, bottles, rocks, trashcans, finally a parking meter crashed the windows and door. Cheers went up. A sort of wooden wall blocking out the front plate glass window was forced down. Then with the parking meter a ram, in went the door. Vengeance vented against the source of repression—gay bars, busts, kids victimized and exploited by the mafia and cops. Strangely, no one spoke to the crowd or tried to direct the insurrection. Everyone's heads were in the same place.

The riots continued for several days on Christopher Street and in other parts of the Village. Supported by local residents and a few tourists they marked the first real time when homosexuals displayed a power that no one could ignore. Those days marked the beginning of Gay liberation.

excerpted from The Politics of Homosexuality by Toby Marotta

George DeSantis

Since the original Parade came down Fifth Aven Washington Square in 1970 (photo at right), hundreds of thousands of gay men and lesbians marched and millions of New Yorkers have wat approving and disapproving. For a liberation da which had such a violent beginning the march h always been very peaceful. There are an estimate one million gay men and lesbians in the greater York area and many turn out "with pride" for th parade or the street festivities afterwards.

Biggart

Best play of the year, 1984, went to Harvey Fierstein who was Grand Marshall of the parade.

1990 Photo by Laura Leeds.

1984 photo by Gail Grieg.

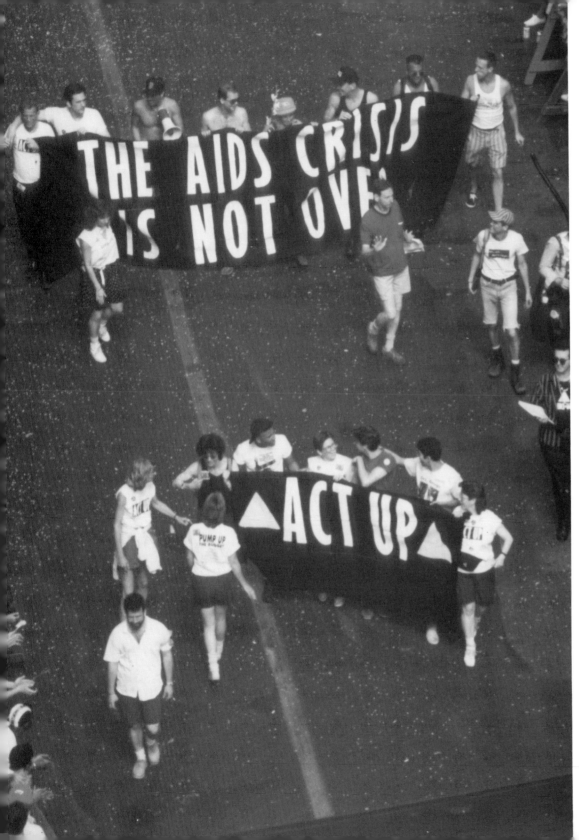

250,000 MARCH IN GAY PARADE
trumpeted the headline in the Daily News.

The devastation of AIDS and increasing violence against gays and lesbians plus the awareness that it is normal not to be completely "straight" combined to form the emotional catalyst needed to bring out the largest numbers ever for the Twentieth Anniversary in 1990. Peaceful as always and led by Mayor Dinkins, the march culminated at the foot of Christopher with a huge dance on the pier. Fireworks were a spectacular finale to this Independence Day.

Photo by Laura Leeds.

AUTHORS

"I have a rendevous with Death
At some disputed barricade,
when Spring comes back with rustling shade
and apple-blossoms fill the air—
I have a rendevous with Death
When Spring comes back blue days and fair."

—Alan Seeger

The poet Alan Seeger often strode the streets in a full-length black cloak and velvet trousers. Dubbed the "Mad Monk of Greenwich Village" by his fellow bohemians, who declared that he "courted Death like a desperate Lover", he joined the toughest branch of the French Foreign Legion and died defending Liberty at a bridge in France during the Somme Offensive on July 4, 1916.

At right—World War I Memorial, Abingdon Square "Defending the Flag", by Phillip Marinez, 1921. (He also did the monument in Chelsea Park)

H. Kaplan

Almost all of America's major authors from 1800-1970 have worked in Greenwich Village. A few, like Henry James and Edith Wharton have been born to riches here. But most came penniless, drawn by the magic of the name *Greenwich Village*—non-natives whose lives were written against the background of its tangled streets. A few came to die.

The author of the *Rights of Man*, Thomas Paine, ended his stormy career here in June of 1809, succored by Madame Bonneville in a cottage near the corner of Bleecker and Grove Streets. More than a century later Sarah Teasdale snuffed out her own life on another corner in an apartment high above Washington Square—number One Fifth Avenue.

But most thrived on the intense intellectual comaraderie that prodded the development of such greats as Eugene O'Neill and Tennessee Williams. The Village even offered sanctuary to those like Herman Melville who felt their careers had failed.

On these pages is a list of most of the authors and playwrights who have worked here and the addresses where they lived.

Samuel Clemens at home at No. 4 West Tenth Street.

Franklin P. Adams .... 250 West 13th Street

James Agee .... 172 Bleecker Street
17 King Street
38 Perry Street

Edward Albee .... 50 West 10th Street
238 West 4th Street

Louisa May Alcott .... 130 MacDougal Street

Margaret Anderson .... 50 West 16th Street

Sherwood Anderson .... 54 Washington Place
12 St. Lukes Place

Louis Auchincloss .... 49 Grove Street

James Baldwin .... 82 Washington Place
Sullivan Street

Djuna Barnes .... No. 5 Patchin Place

Stephen Vincent Benet .... Seven Arts

William Rose Benet .... 75 Washington Place
36 West 9th Street

Underwood and Underwood

Maxwell Bodenheim......................34 Washington Square

William Cullen Bryant.....................24 West 16th Street
12 Carmine Street

William Burroughs.................................San Remo Bar

Willa Cather...........................82 Washington Place
5 Bank Street

Samuel Clemens.........................4 West 10th Street
(Mark Twain)

Hart Crane...............................25 East 11th Street
54 West 10th Street
139 East 15th Street
45 Grove Street
24 West 16th Street

Stephen Crane.................61 Washington Square South

James Fenimore Cooper....................145 Bleecker Street
No. 4 Carroll Place

Gregory Corso...........................190 Bleecker Street

e.e. cummings..........................No. 4 Patchin Place
21 East 15th Street
11 Christopher Street
9 West 14th Street

Richard Harding Davis....................108 Waverly Place

Floyd Dell............................91 Greenwich Avenue

Mark Van Doren............................43 Barrow Street
393 Bleecker Street

Theodore Dreiser..............................Mills Hotel
16 St. Lukes Place
118 West 11th Street

Max Eastman...............................137 MacDougal
91 Greenwich Avenue

T.S. Eliot.............................No. 4 Patchin Place

Ralph Waldo Emerson..........................Pfaff's Tavern

James T. Farrell..............................Brevoort Hotel

Robert Frost..................................Seven Arts

Carl Paler

Edgar Allen Poe completed an idea given to him by a friend when he wrote "The Bells" here on Amity Street, while he listened to the bells of the Village churches. Perhaps his most famous poem, "The Raven", was also first released from here.

Thomas Wolfe—Of Time and the River—found his "first decent apartment" here on West 11th Street.

Edward Albee found the perfect title when he saw "Who's Afraid of Virginia Woolf?" scrawled in lipstick across a mirror in the basement of this bar. (According to the neighbors this bar is now a notorious "hustler" bar owned and operated by the syndicate.)

Kahil Gibran . . . . 51 West 10th Street

Allen Ginsberg . . . . East Village

Williams Glackens . . . . 3 Washington Square No.

E.L. Godkin . . . . 38 West 10th Street

Bret Harte . . . . 16 Fifth Avenue
713 Broadway
487 Hudson Street

Washington Irving . . . . No. 11 Commerce Street

Henry James . . . . 21 Washington Place
11 Fifth Avenue
57 West 14th Street
27 Waverly Place

James Jones . . . . 49 Grove Street

Mary Cadwalader Jones . . . . 21 East 11th Street

Harry Kemp . . . . Patchin Place

Rockwell Kent . . . . San Remo Bar
149 West 21st Street

Emma Lazarus . . . . 18 West 10th Street

Sinclair Lewis . . . . 17 West 10th Street
137 MacDougal Street

Vachel Lindsay . . . . 137 MacDougal Street

Walter Lippmann . . . . Seven Arts

Jack London . . . . Washington Square South

Norman Mailer . . . . White Horse Tavern

John Masefield . . . . Corner Christopher and
Greenwich Avenue
(Columbia Gardens)

Mary McCarthy . . . . 18 Gay Street

Ruth McKenney . . . . 14 Gay Street

Herman Melville . . . . 33 Bleecker Street
675 Broadway
Gansevoort Street Wharf

No. 751/2 Bedford Street, "The narrowest house in the Village", was once the home of Edna St. Vincent Millay and John Barrymore, at different times of course.

Washington Irving's house at No. 11 Commerce Street where he is purported to have written much of "The Legend of Sleepy Hollow."

Carl Paler

Edna St. Vincent Millay	25 Charlton Street
	75½ Bedford Street
	139 Waverly Place
Merle Miller	49 Grove Street
Clement Clarke Moore	St. Lukes In the Fields
Marianne Moore	35 West 9th Street
	14 St. Lukes Place
Anais Nin	215 West 13th Street
Frank Norris	61 Washington Square South
Eugene O'Neill	38 Washington Square
	133 MacDougal Street
Thomas Paine	59 Grove Street
John Dos Passos	75 Washington Place
	3 Washington Square North
Edgar Allen Poe	85 Amity Place
	(West 3rd Street)
	18 Amity Place
	Corner 6th Avenue and Waverly
	113½ Carmine Street
William Sydney Porter (O. Henry)	61 Washington Square South
Ezra Pound	No. 4 Patchin Place
John Reed	147 West 4th Street
	42 Washington Square South
	No. 7 Patchin Place
Edward Arlington Robinson	61 Washington Square South
	121 Washington Place
Carl Sandburg	91 Greenwich Avenue
Alan Seeger	61 Washington Square South
Upton Sinclair	37 MacDougal Street
Lincoln Stephens	42 Washington Square South
William Styron	49 Grove Street
	75 West 11th Street
	45 Greenwich Avenue

Ida Tarbell...................34 Washington Square	Walt Whitman...........................Pfaff's Tavern
Allen Tate......................27 Bank Street	Tennessee Williams......................Greenwich Street
Sara Teasdale...................No. 1 Fifth Avenue	Edmund Wilson.....................114 West 16th Street
William Thackeray................57 West 14th Street	3 Washington Square North
Scofield Thayer.................152 West 13th Street	No. 1 University Place
James Thurber...........Horatio and Greenwich Streets	Thomas Wolfe.........................Hotel Albert
Gore Vidal......................49 Grove Street	(University Place & East 11th Street)
Nathaniel West....................Brevoort Hotel	27 West 15th Street
E.B. White.....................West 13th Street	263 West 11th Street
	Richard Wright....................82 Washington Place
	Elinor Wylie.....................75 Washington Place
	36 West 9th Street

Ladies Home Journal, December, 1898.

The Alcott home is still standing at 130 MacDougal Street.

DRAWN BY H. C. IRELAND   MAY ALCOTT   LOUISA ALCOTT   MR. ALCOTT   MRS. ALCOTT   ANNA ALCOTT

The Fantasticks was first presented by Lore Noto at the Sullivan Street Playhouse, New York City, on May 3rd, 1960, with the following cast: *The Mute, Richard Stauffer; El Gallo, Jerry Orbach; Luisa, Rita Gardner; Matt, Kenneth Nelson; Hucklebee, William Larsen; Bellomy, Hugh Thomas; Henry, Thomas Bruce; Mortimer, George Curley; The Handyman, Jay Hampton; The Pianist, Julian Stein; The Harpist, Beverly Mann; Director, Word Baker; Musical Director and Arrangements, Julian Stein; Production Designer, Ed Wittstein.*

THEATRE!

The Long Voyage Home, by Eugene O'Neill. Nov. 2, 1917. Playwright's Theatre. Performed in repertory with the other one-act plays. Prod.: The Provincetown Players. Dir.: Nina Moise. Set: Ira Remson. A saloon on the Thames waterfront. The sailor Olson (Irma Remson), who has made enough money on the *Glencairn* to leave the sea and buy farm land in Sweden, is drugged and "crimped" (shanghaied). The whore Freda (Ida Rauh) hands his money to the saloonkeeper Fat Joe (George Cram Cook). Cook, himself a playwright and husband of the playwright Susan Glaspell, was one of the founders and directors of the Provincetown Players. (Photo: Paul Thompson)

The Ridiculous Theatrical Company, founded in 1987 with Charles Ludlam (le[as artistic director and playwright-in-residence, has developed a style of ensemble playing that synthesizes wit, parody, vaudeville farce, melodrama a satire, giving reckless immediacy to classical stagecraft.

With Mr. Ludlam's passing in 1987, **Everett Quinton** became artistic directo Seen above in Georg Osterman's 1990 adaptation of Dr. Jekyll and Mr. Hyde an with Charles in the 1984 presentation of The Mystery Of Irma Vep, Mr. Quinto has garnered critical acclaim and enhanced the company's international reputation. The ensemble continues to present revivals of Mr. Ludlam's classic madcap frivolities and new seasons of original work. (photos by Shevett)

Charles Ludlam in 1984 by Harvey Kaplan.

"I love the theatre!" exclaimed **Ron Kovic**, *author of the Academy Award winning* Born on the Fourth of July, *as he was surrounded in 1985 by the all-female cast and crew of* Home on the Range *at the Courtyard Playhouse.*

(below) **Edith O'Hara,** *guiding light of the* **Thirteenth Street Repertory Company,** *has emerged from her basement playhouse since 1972.* *Israel Horowitz'* LINE, *the longest running off-off Broadway play, has been going strong since 1975.*

Photos by Gaylord.

ENTERTAINMENT

Tito Puente as he appeared on stage at the original free opening concert in Washington Square for the 1970 Village Jazz Festival.

"Jazz needs the Night" and nearly twenty-one thousand nights have passed fulfilled since The Village Vanguard opened its doors on Charles Street. One year later, Max Gordon moved the club to its present location at 176 Seventh Avenue South. Dozens of poets such as Maxwell Bodenheim, John Rose Gildea, and Harry Kemp recited verse and verbiage long before the Beatniks of the fifties. "Pop" singers Harry Belefonte, Barbra Streisand and Dinah Washington and folk singers The Weavers, Josh White, Leadbelly and Woody Guthrie warbled their tunes here, many for their first big chance. Comedians Judy Holliday, Betty Comden, Adolph Green, Woody Allen and Pearl Bailey wowed them first at the Vanguard or The Blue Angel (Max's uptown club for two decades). And after he switched to a jazz format, virtually every member of the Kingdom of Jazz from Miles Davis to Charles Mingus has played here.

Born in Vilna in Lithuania Mr. Gordon "maximised" the virtues and talents of America. His final thoughts on the Vanguard says it all. "After running a place for as many years as I have, you discover that your place takes on a life of its own after awhile. You started it, you put your ideas into it, your hopes and your dreams. It's your baby, but now its got a life of its own, and you better know it."

An entity unto itself, both legend and reality, Max's Village Vanguard sits waiting on this night and for many, many nights to come.

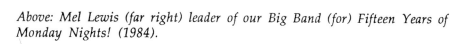

Above: Mel Lewis (far right) leader of our Big Band (for) Fifteen Years of Monday Nights! (1984).

Above right: **Miles Davis** *when he was a kid. This is how he looked when he came to New York, playing for the first time in the big city. That's* **Roy Haynes** *on drums.*

Right: The Revuers, four of them (left to right in 1939): **Adolph Green, Judy Holliday, Betty Comden and Alvin Hammer.** *They look so young and handsome. This is how they looked, just coming in off the street in their street clothes--rehearsing or auditioning. Judy was so beautiful, and they were all nice kids.* **(Captions from Live at the Village Vanguard, 1980, Max Gordon)**

ASTI'S

Adolph Mariani founded this restaraunt cum opera house at 13 East 12th Street in 1926. In the 1930's it was a favorite haunt of Arturo Toscanini and over the years, judging from the autographed photos on the walls, was visited by all the major opera stars in the world. After 60 years the mixture of grand opera and comedy is still as fresh and exciting as ever. Everybody sings! Below left: Singing son, Augusto Mariani. Center: Maria Fattore tempts Vittorio Ciepiel. Right: Pasquale Pugliese.

Adolph Mariani and Noel Coward.

Entertainment, Street Division.

Father Demo Square is so peaceful in the Springtime near Our Lady of Pompeii Church that one can almost forget the continual roar of Sixth Avenue. But sometime late in July...

....the *Festa Italiana* occurs.

Rocco Galitioto

Carmine Street explodes with activity as a midway appears
complete with games, tons of food and even a ferris wheel!

Gaylord

Steven Bloomfield

St. Anthony's Festival

FOOD! *The most important draw for any Italian Street Festival*

Top: Carl Paler
Right: Jack Berger

H. Kaplan

Ye Olde Village Fair, grandmother of all the block parties, has been held every May in and around the intersections of Commerce, Barrow and Bedford Streets since 1975. Over 200 vendors and live entertainment make it a joyous occasion. Many locals occupy booths and the middle-of-the street cafe is a great place to people-watch.

All of the profits from this fair are donated to local charities. Cecily Fortescue, a local potter, displays her wares in front of the historic Cherry Lane Theatre, founded in 1924 by Edna St. Vincent Millay.

The Christopher Street Merchant's Association holds its fair simultaneously with Ye Olde Village Fair. This triumvirate holds sway over the display for The Village Men's Shop which has been located here on Christopher since 1947 (lower right).

P. S. 41, on Greenwich Avenue (below) holds a flea market every Saturday (weather permitting) with an enormous variety of goods.
Mini-Flea Markets like the puppet sale at top right abound on the side streets in summer.

William Acker

Gaylord

Street Entertainers

*I*t is without any hesitation that New Yorker's boast that the musicians that appear on their streets are usually better than those that appear in most cities concert halls. Every type of performer appears at random on almost every corner of the Village in the summertime and a few struggle through their melodies in the winter.

The Hurdy-Gurdy Man.

Ancient sounds seem to fill Bleecker Street as Donald Heller plays a hundred-year-old hurdy gurdy. Since 1978 he often performs with his wife Anicet, whom he met while studying at the National Puppet Theatre in Budapest.

Carl Paler

Gaylord

Carl Paler

A seemingly angelic cellist and an anonymous japanese violinist become a classical duet on opposite sides of Bleecker Street.

Mamoo the Clown on his unicycle with 14 foot boa constrictor, Big Ben.

Dancers on Greenwich Avenue.

Tap dancers perform in front of Christopher Park during the renovation of 1984-85.

HALLOWEEN PARADE

An Eighteenth Century Balladeer seems to be summoning the spirits of Halloween from Union Square, amidst painted pumpkins in the gathering dusk. (Linda Russell-Photo by Gaylord.)

The Greenwich Village Halloween Parade has grown from an artists' project that snaked through the West Village from Westbeth to a late-night saturnalia in Washington Square. Now the revelers have grown in number to close to a million and the route commences on Houston Street and drives straight through to Union Square.

The soft-shoe dancer from Hell moves sand for pennies at Sheridan Square. ▶

Photos by Gaylord

Wm. Acker

A delightful and safe time for children.

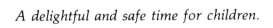

left: Attitude Galore, by Bill Biggart

Above: A frightened-looking little Village witch posed for the photographer of The Burr McIntosh Monthly *in 1909.*

ENTERTAINMENT: ANIMAL DIVISION

See the Antique Cat.
See how the eyes seem
to follow you everywhere.
Just like a Real Cat.

Bleecker Street by William Acker.

Sam and his son Max stand guard over the beauteous pug Natasha as the proprietor of RS Antiques at 11 Christopher looks on. There will always be some question as to whether this trio is his owner or vice versa.

In 1945 there were more than 25,000 dogs in Greenwich Village and as the Village Tattler put it "God only knows how many cats". Today there are many, many more animals here that bring joy to their owners and to friendly passers-by.

102

Carl Paler

Stone dog on West Tenth Street

The corner building housing the White Horse Tavern was built in 1817. Dylan Thomas, the Welsh poet, was a very frequent visitor before he died in the old main building of St. Vincents Hospital.

Susan Maytell

Lions lurk on West 11th and on Bank Streets (photos by Carl Paler).
Animals Galore charm children on West Eighth Street. (Bottom photos by William Acker)

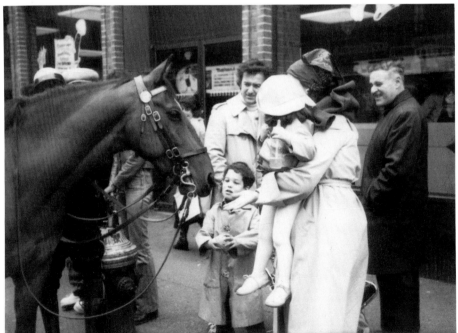

Entertainment: Business Division.

Although continually threatened by the "New Greed," the businessmen and women of the Village manage to survive and provide the most diversified shopping area in New York City.

Stanley Coren of Greenwich Avenue's Beige Gallery originally comes from England but his wares come from America's past.

Mr. Lianides founded The Coach House in 1949 and it soon became a favorite dining spot for the late and magnificent James Beard of West Tenth Street.

Typical of the diverse population of the Village, the staff of Chez Michallet forms a line of white in front of this cozy restaurant on the corner of Bedford and Grove Streets (left).
left to right: Gerrit Vooren originally from Amsterdam, Holland; Dan Lanier--Appalachicola, Florida; Stephane Michallet-Ferrier--Grenoble France; Andreas Vasquez--Mexico City, Mexico; Kazuo Suzuki--Tokyo, Japan; Jessica Michallet-Ferrier-- Grenoble, France; and Norma Bogdon--born in Brooklyn, USA.

Christopher Kosmas paints modern-day icons in his West Tenth Street studio. some of his many pieces are hung in St. Johns Church on Eleventh Street.

William Acker, photographer, had his digs on West Eighth Street for more than forty of his ninety years. His family has lived in the Village since 1870 (see photo of his grandfather's store in 1880 on the following page).

The photo at top left on the following page is of "Salvatore's La Licata Market" at the corner of Perry and Washington Streets in 1910, that catered to the Spanish sailors from schooners on West Street. Salvatore was the uncle of Angelo Bonsanque, the present owner of North Pole Meats shown in 1953 (far right) the southeast corner of Bleecker and Christopher. In 1890 this same store was owned and operated as a dry goods store by the grandfather of photographer William Acker. The North Pole is now located at 514 Hudson Street and the Bleecker Street corner is a Korean Deli.

*O*ne of the nicest things about the Village is its continuity of business. The building at left was built in 1873 to house a liquor store in the rear. The owner/builder also lived upstairs here at the corner of Waverly Place and Sixth Avenue.

The house below was built in 1802 with a grocery store in mind. Originally an all-frame building, the Commissioners Plan of 1807-1811 was mapped out on its second floor.

Carl Paler

In the middle background below is St. John's Evangelical Lutheran Church built in 1852 in the Federal Style. The Hartwick Seminary was on this site in 1792 and catacombs from this date still exist beneath the church. *1948 Photo by William Acker.*

The corner of Bleecker and Christopher in 1880, William Acker's grandfather is at left.

Anthony Zito fired up the brick ovens of this famous bakery for the first time on December 14, 1924. Now run by his son, all of the immediate employees are members of the Zito family.

photo by Steven Bloomfield

Carl Paler

Gail Chisholm of Chisholm Gallery and Joseph Markus of Starstruck Vintage Clothing have for over a decade set the style for Greenwich Avenue

Expectant customers line up outside Lilac Chocolates on Christopher. At the same family-owned location since 1923, presently managed by Martha and Ed Bond.

Bill Cunningham

Carl Paler

Bruce and Charlotte Mager have struck a happy note by specializing in vintage American radio and recording equipment at Waves on East Thirteenth Street.

Ta-daa! Proprietors Liz Howe and Ellen Enke present Mrs. Hudson's Video Library on....where else? Hudson Street.

Right: John's Pizza of Bleecker Street was started in 1934. The Thunderbird in 1957. (Steven Bloomfield)

John's
John's
THE ORIGINAL BRICK OVEN PIZZA
JOHN'S
PIZZERIA
PORT'ALBA
WINES-BEER
280

Upper left: *The block as it appears today.*

Above: *Bigelow's Pharmacy in 1895.*

Left: *Kaiser's Mens Shop in the 1940's.*

Bigelow's originally started in 1868 in the building now occupied by Kaiser's Mens Wear (see photos at left). When Bigelow's moved to their newly constructed building two doors down, in 1902, Kaiser's moved in. The original marble floor from 1868 is still in place.

This cartoon appeared in the **Village Bugle,** July, 1939.

DRESSING UP

Village Square, taken from the roof of the old Nedick's Building (now B. Dalton Bookseller), after the demolition of the Sixth Avenue Elevated in 1939. The esthetically awful Women's Prison (above right center) built in 1929 with the protection of the corrupt Jimmy Walker administration was not demolished until 1969. (See Photo of Jefferson Market and the "el" on page 22.)

Mayor La Guardia expressing his pleasure at signing the bill naming Village Square.
(*William A. Kaiser is shaking hands with the Mayor in this November 9, 1939*
photo from The Villager)

On December 11, 1939, the mayor helped plant the first of three Oriental plane trees on the east side of Sixth Avenue between Eighth and Ninth Streets to beautify the area after the el was demolished (many have since been removed but one tree planted at this time can be seen across the street by the Jefferson Market Garden). Fifth Avenue had received its trees in December, 1935, and six trees were planted around the new Schraffts Building at the southeast corner of Thirteenth and Fifth. Cecil Silber, owner of No. One Christopher planted trees in front of his new apartment house at about the same time (three of which are still standing). All were Oriental Plane trees.

By 1850 the Common Council of New York was so corrupt that its members were referred to as "the forty thieves" and the moment was ripe for William H. (Boss) Tweed and the Tammany Society to take command. When he was elected as the head of Tammany Hall in 1863 he was quick to control the police force and install crooked judges.

He managed to block construction of a subway line in 1868, and was outraged when Ely Beach opened the first subway in 1870 (the tunnel was clandestinely dug by its inventor and ran on pneumatic power). All further plans for subways were shelved until after Tweed's fall from power and subsequent death in Ludlow Street Jail in 1872. By then the Elevated Railway had arrived. The first "el" was patented by Charles Harvey and completed up Greenwich Street and Ninth Avenue from the Battery to the railway terminal at 30th Street in Chelsea on July 2, 1867.

The Sixth Avenue El was begun in 1876 and completed by June, 1878.

By the early 1890's the elevateds began to deteriorate and the long-planned subways were begun. The Independent Rapid Transit Line up Third Avenue reached Union Square in 1904 and in 1913 a contract was let to construct a line down Seventh Avenue from a crosstown line already built at 42nd Street. On July 1, 1918, it was completed to the Battery. First-hand accounts by Villagers recall having to cross the "open pit" construction on wooden planks as it passed Bleecker Street in 1916. Seventh Avenue South had already been broadened and run through to Varick.

Actual construction of the Eighth Avenue Line began at 123rd street on March 14, 1925, and worked its way down Eighth Avenue to West Fourteenth Street and across Greenwich Avenue to Sixth Avenue and West Fourth. It was officially opened on September 10, 1932. On January 1, 1936, Mayor La Guardia opened the Houston Street line and the Sixth Avenue Subway was completed down from West 53rd to West Fourth Street on December 14, 1940.

The Sixth Avenue "el" was not completely demolished until March 23, 1939, and the scrap metal was sold to the Japanese much to the dismay of many New Yorkers just two years before Pearl Harbor.

Right: Bleecker Street at night, by Laura Leeds.

Carl Paler

Mike and his intelligent friend Bwana, operate briefly on West Fourth street.

Olmeca Lori Washington stops to display her handmade jewelry on Seventh Avenue. Crafts, especially jewelry, are ripe targets for the police.

Gaylord

Mike "Eagle" Kennick, the last of the basement booksellers, closed his used book store in 1990. Many one-man book stores like his have proliferated in the Village for decades. Twelve years of misadministration has forced them all out.

Many small-decades-old businesses have closed or moved out of Manhattan because of sky-rocketing rents and the lack of some sort of control over commercial leases.

HOMELESS AND FRIENDLESS.

THE DISCARDED POOR

Although conditions for the homeless poor have improved greatly since this etching of a boy in Jones Street was made in 1884, city officials, police and private citizens continue to harrass them and, which is far worse, try to forget they exist. Every walk through the parks and streets of New York City provides views of the discarded human beings who lie on street corners or huddle for warmth in doorways. Primitive shelters provided by the city offer little refuge and are sometimes far more dangerous than the streets. These photos were all taken in Greenwich Village, affluent Greenwich Village, whose Community Boards, elected officials and, sadly enough, a majority of its residents, tend to treat these people as dangerous nuisances.

These shoe shine boys come
out of the slowly shrinking ghetto
of Chelsea near the projects
on Ninth Avenue.

14th St. and 8th Ave. by Jack Berger

Flo Fox

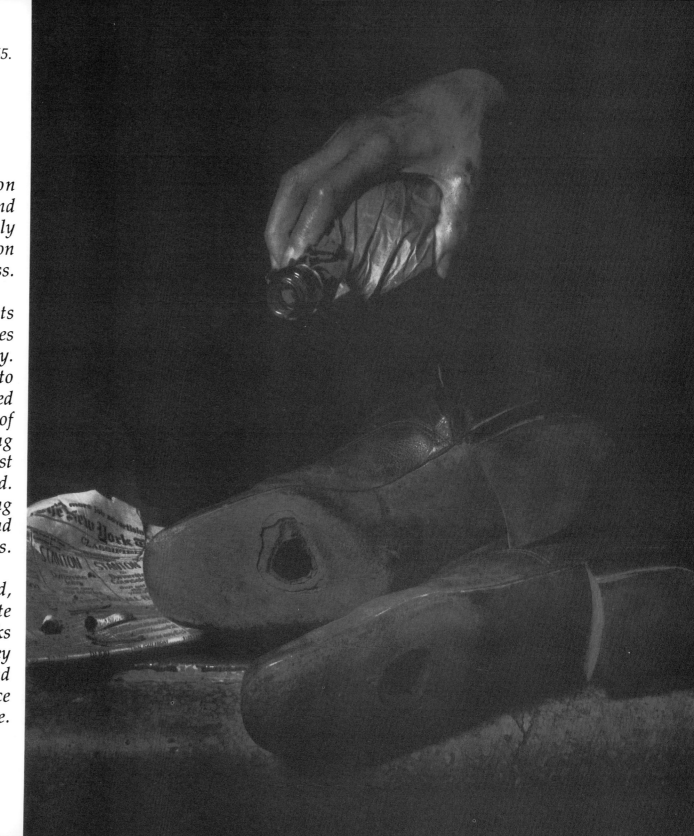

Desolation
Despair and
Loneliness only
add to the degradation
of being homeless.

Some choose the streets
to avoid the confines
of a money oriented society.
But most have been forced into
this situation by the continued
gentrification of areas of
affordable housing
or their own inability to exist
in the "normal" world.
They stumble. searching
for their former ties and
future dreams.

The young, the very old,
the helpless and the desperate
crowd the streets and parks
of the Village, falling prey
to the insults, ignorance and
sometimes violence
of local citizens and the Police.

*I*n April of 1985, famous comedienne Lucille Ball disguised her beauty to portray an elderly bag lady for the TV film *Stone Pillow*. This poignant story pointed to the desperate plight of the many homeless that literally live in the streets of our Village. This scene was shot on Bleecker Street near Abingdon Square Park, a sometimes hangout for older street people.

Photos by Geoffrey Dahlberg

His livingroom is Christopher Street.

Gaylord

The lady pictured above wrote the following letter to help raise funds for **The Village Visiting Neighbors, 135 West Fourth Street (260-6200).**

I'd like to introduce myself to you. My name is Emily Law and I'm 81 year old. O'h I'm not complaining—in fact I'm grateful to be alive and kicking and especially grateful for Village Visiting Neighbors and all the manynew people I've met through them since my husband died three years ago.

I met John through Village Visiting Neighbors. He started to visit me shortly after my husband died. I was feeling very depressed and lonely. And there he was, a young man coming to *visit me!* We've been laughing, telephoning and sharing together ever since. Sundays are extra-special. John comes over with croissants or coffeecake. We talk non-stop. His visits mean the world to me

Village Visiting Neighbors is committed to helping seniors like me—people who are homebound or need some assistance so we can continue to live in our own homes. Without Village Visiting Neighbors many of us would end up in institutions or hospitals.

The Caring Community, 7 West 11th Street (675-2257) is a coalition of churches, synagogues, and social service agencies in the Greenwich Village area. We banded together in 1973 as individuals and professionals concerned about the quality of life in our community.

Today, the Caring Community sponsors four centers in Greenwich Village. These centers provide nutritional, recreational, social and health services to senior citizens. But we do more than that. A major goal is to provide senior citizens with a sense of family. We provide the friendless with friends, the isolated with a sense of belonging, and all with a spirit of community in its true sense.

STREET INDEX

STREET BY

The good New York City Councilmen who met in 1794 to change most of the British names of local streets to appropriate American ones also begrudgingly decided to keep the old plan of naming the streets at the outer boundaries of the city Art Street and Science Street. They thought it possible to cling to this old plan since, obviously, it would take centuries for the city to grow much farther than the proposed Parade at what is now 14th Street. They had a neat and tidy plan: to number the streets running north and south, beginning with Broadway and working west to Greenwich Street (which would be Eighth Street under this plan).

As to the city's growth, however, they could not have foreseen the tremendous physical expansion caused by the Yellow Fever epidemics which began in 1798, for at that time it was thought that the fever inhered to certain locations, rather than being transmitted by some germ which could be carried by humans when they moved; thus flight was considered the best preventative measure. And as to the rigid grid plan they planned for the city, they had overlooked the obstinacy and independence of Villagers, already manifesting itself in their point-blank refusal to acknowledge the new numbering system while they hewed to the old names given to their streets.

By 1807, slightly over a decade later, the city's population had grown to 83,530. An enormous influx of immigrants, the changing demographics caused by the flight from the fever, and the generally rag-tag construction that went with these factors caused the City Council to decide that it had to do something to give direction to what up to this point had been wildly undisciplined growth.

The Commissioners Plan of 1807-11 was to number streets running east and west—beginning with Bleecker Street (as First Street); all avenues would progress first in alphabetical order (A, B, C, etc.). It looked good on paper; it made good sense above 14th Street; but it caused rampant consternation and confusion among bewildered Villagers, who have never been shy about showing their displeasure for what they perceive as the general idiocy of city fathers, urban planners and other such bureaucratic figures.

To the east, between Broadway and Sixth Avenue, the population was about to be faced with two identical numbering systems—the old system running north to south, the new one east to west. To the west of Sixth Avenue, Villagers were aghast at the thought of converting to numbered streets in any direction. The general reaction of Villagers was "Thanks, but no thanks"—a tradition of resistance to what many call "progress" that continues to this day (and probably accounts for the fact that alone among New York neighborhoods, the Village preserves a feeling of human scale and cohesive historical identity).

In the map section that follows you will be able to trace the changes in street names. Remember that while most British names were changed following the Revolutionary War, a few English "ghettos" remained. Interestingly, fashion dictated for a time that all streets named for local property owners were to carry the first name only. I guess that everyone felt that the owners were locally famous enough that further description was unnecessary.

Perry Street in the snow.

Many aesthetic questions have been raised about the Commissioners Plan of 1807-11, which required the palisades of Manhattan to be dynamited, hills bulldozed and the entire island generally "regulated" (graded to one level). The monotonous combination of nearly flat surfaces and a severely organized, rigid grid of streets and avenues surely could have done with the relief of a few ovals, and even one of the Commissioners deplored the lack of green.

The Commissioners, of course, had not the prescience to realize the effect of their arrangement on future generations. In a grid, neighborhoods exist arbitrarily. Such neighborhoods represent not so much humanity as mathematics. When the people move, their history moves on with them. The sterility of any such numbering system isolates the individual and deprives him or her of the basic human need to identify, name and control the environment.

Fortunately, Greenwich Village existed before the grid, and the city's northward drive eddied and swirled around it when the Commissioners Plan was implemented. One of the best and most lasting effects of this comparative isolation from the progress attendant upon city growth was the Village's opportunity to preserve its history in the names of our streets.

The Village has been from the beginning essentially an "American" community, and each successive nationality or group has proudly named parks and streets for its own heros and leaders and its own history—a history which itself comprises and mirrors the early, larger history of the United States, much of which has quite literally been acted out on Village doorsteps.

The Following compendium of named streets and the explanation of numbered streets which follows will give you a brief glimpse of the past 280 sometimes very odd years in Greenwich Village.

Flo Fox

A COMPENDIUM OF GREENWICH VILLAGE STREET NAMES— OLD AND NEW.

Abingdon Place—former name of part of West 12th St. between Abingdon Square and Greenwich Ave.

Abingdon Square—the triangle bounded by Eighth Ave. and Hudson and West 12th Sts., named prior to 1779 for the Earl of Abingdon, son-in-law of Admiral Sir Peter Warren (see History).

Amity Lane—laid out on the West Bayard farm in 1752, it followed the approximate course of present West Fourth St. from Broadway to MacDougal St. and was sometimes referred to as East Herring.

Amity Street—former name of West Third St., sometimes referred to as Amity Place; originally laid out in 1806 from Broadway to MacDougal St.

Amos Street—named for Richard Amos, who ceded the land to the city in 1809, it was opened in 1815 from Greenwich Lane to the Hudson River. It became part of West 10th St. in 1857. Christopher, Charles and Amos Sts. were all named for members of one large family of landowners (Christopher and Charles Sts. for Christopher Charles Amos, and Amos for Richard.)

Ardens Street—former name of part of Morton Street between Herring (Bleecker) Street and the Episcopal churchyard.

Art Street—former name of the "road to the Monument" or Sand Hill Road, it ran from the Bowery to join Greenwich Lane at approximately the site of future Sixth Ave. Before the Commissioners Plan of 1807-11 it was to be paired with Science St., to run across present-day Washington Square. Art St. was regulated in 1808, then closed between Sixth Ave. and Broadway in 1825; the last little tail became Astor Place in 1840. Science St. was never begun.

Astor Place—the end of Art St. from Broadway to the Bowery: named for John Jacob Astor, "the richest man in America," eight years before his death in 1848.

Asylum Street—laid out as Chester St. by the powers-that-be prior to 1779, this lane connected the scattered estates and farms that comprised the West Village and was known locally as William St. (q.v.; for William W. Gilbert, through whose lands it passed). When the New York Orphan Asylum was built this street began to be referred to as "the road to the Asylum" along its entire length from the end of present West Forth St. to the Great Kill Road (Gansevoort St.). Its name was changed to West Fourth St. in 1833.

Avenue of the Americas—named for the Organization of American States, New Yorkers refuse to call it anything but Sixth Ave. Consternation and near tragedy occurred when Police Emergency computers refused to respond after being programmed for "Avenue of the Americas" rather than Sixth Ave. After many years of confusion the city has finally put *both* names on street corners.

Bank street—unnamed prior to 1799, the short stretch between Hudson St. and the river became known unofficially as Bank St. when the Bank of New York, fleeing the Yellow Fever epidemics (see History), opened a branch there in 1798. It was officially laid out in 1807.

Barrow Street—laid out as Reason St. prior to 1799 (in honor of Thomas Paine's *The Age of Reason*), unimpressed locals soon corrupted it to "Raisin" St. — "raisin" being a euphemism for a black slave. When William W. Gilbert and his wife, together with Trinity Church, ceded it to the city in 1808-1809, the church hastened to have it rechristened in honor of artist Thomas Barrow, famed for his beatific portrayal of Trinity Church in 1807.

Bayard Place—formerly part of Greenwich St. Between Jane and Horatio Sts.; named for the Bayard family house which stood until 1890.

Bedford Street—laid out prior to 1799 and named for Bedford St. in London (see also Downing St.).

Bethune Street—opened in 1827 and named for the charitable Mrs. Johanna Graham Bethune, the early 19th-century philanthropist and educator who founded, with Mrs. Alexander Hamilton, the New York Orphan Asylum.

Bleecker Street—originally, Bleecker ran only from Bowery Road to Broadway opposite David St. It was ceded to the city by Anthony L. Bleecker in 1805; he also ceded David St. in 1809 and 1812. Eventually the entire length from Bowery to Carmine St. became known as Bleecker St., although not until the late 19th century did it engulf Herring St. and stretch to its present conclusion at Hudson St. (see also David and Herring Sts.; Carrol Place and DePau Row).

Brannon Street—former name for Spring St., laid out prior to 1799, Brannon St. was ceded to the city by Trinity Church. It was extended west of Washington St. in 1803; the name was changed to Spring St. (q.v.) in 1807.

Broadway—was a mere Indian path prior to 1609, became *Heerwegh* or *Heere Straet* under Dutch rule, and came into its present title late in 1668 after the British invaded. Called Great Gorge St. from Ann St. to Sand Hill Road (Astor Place) in 1775, not until 1794 was it considered one continuous roadway with one name, Broadway.

Brook Street—former name of Hancock Street (q.v.); probably named for Minetta Brook (Bestavaars Creek) which ran down the middle of present day Sixth Ave. from Bleecker and Minetta Sts. and into the Hudson near Charlton St.

Windmill on Jane Street at Eighth Avenue.

H. Kaplan

The First Public Library in the Village, at 13th Street and Greenwich Avenue.

Budd Street—former name of Van Dam St.

Burr Street—former name of Charlton St.

Burrows Street—former name of Grove Street; named for Lt. William Burrows in 1814; see also Cozine and Columbia Sts.

Burton Street—former name of Leroy St. between Herring (Bleecker) St. and the Episcopal Churchyard (see Leroy St.)

Carmine Street—partly laid out and called Germaine St. prior to 1799, it was opened up in 1817 from Bleecker to Warwick Sts., and extended to the river in 1819; named for Nicholas Carman, an early vestryman of Trinity Church, corrupted to Carmine.

Carroll Place—former name of the section of Bleecker St. between South Fifth Ave. (LaGuardia Place) and Thompson St. Home of Samuel F.B. Morse and family from 1833 to 1841 (the building still stands at 145 Bleecker).

Charles Lane—known as "Pig Alley" for obvious reasons (i.e., pigs were kept there) until well into the 20th century; runs a brief and cobbled life from 692 Washington to West St.

Charles Street—laid out prior to 1799 and regulated from Greenwich St. to the State Prison in 1810; see also Van Ness Place.

Charlton Street—originally laid out as Hetty St.; changed to Burr St. for the owner of the property prior to 1799. Additional land was ceded by Trinity Church, opening Charlton St. to the Hudson River in 1806. It was named in 1807 for Dr. John Charlton, an English surgeon who remained after the Revolutionary War and eventually became president of the New York Medical Society.

Christopher Park—a triangle bounded by West Fourth, Christopher and Grove Sts., this recently refurbished parts was named in 1836 but officially designated Greenwich Park in 1856.

Christopher Street—originally called Skinner Road for Colonel William Skinner, a son-in-law of Sir Admiral Peter Warren, this is one of the oldest roadways in the Village to survive in (nearly) its original form, running from a cove on the Hudson River to meet with Greenwich Lane. The street was almost certainly run through prior to 1700; named prior to 1799 for Christopher Charles Amos, a local landowner. (See also Charles and Amos Sts.)

Clarkson Street—ceded by Trinity Church in 1808 as Morton Street (q.v.), it was named for Revolutionary War hero Matthew Clarkson in 1810. (See also Morton St.)

Columbia Street—the original name of Grove St. prior to 1799.

Congress Street—a tiny cross street below Houston St. obliterated when Sixth Ave. was run through from Carmine to Canal St.

Cornelia Street—named for the beloved granddaughter of Robert Herring (he owned the land), and laid out in 1794. (See Herring St.)

Cozine Street—another former name of Grove St.; for a prominent local family until 1814. (See also Burrows and Columbia Sts.)

David Street—former name of part of Bleecker St.

DePau Row—former name of part of Bleecker St, known for its splendid houses.

Dominic Street—namesake unrecorded; former name of Downing St.

Downing Street—partly laid out prior to 1799 and probably named for the London street (as is Bedford). When the Common Council met in 1794 to expunge all British names from the city maps, a few were evidently passed over in deference to citizens of British ancestry still living nearby.

Eliza Street—named for Eliza Fenton, mentioned in letters from Washington Irving to A.L. Bleecker.

Father Demo Square—a rhombus bounded by Sixth Ave., Carmine and Bleecker Sts. Named for an early pastor of Our Lady of Pompei Church, now at Bleecker and Carmine Sts.

Synagogue on Charles Street, erected in 1889.

Factory Street—former name for Waverly Place between Christopher and Bank Sts.; changed in 1853.

Fitzroy Road—followed the present path of Eighth Ave. to Abingdon Road (21st St.); like Abingdon, named for a son-in-law of Admiral Sir Peter Warren; see Great Kill Road.

Gansevoort Street—the very end of Great Kill Road, the Dutch name for the later Fitzroy Road that led to the Great Kill or stream that crossed the island below 42nd St. Locals and some later historians corrupted it to Great Kiln Road to agree with the presence of a large lime kiln near the former site of Fort Gansevoort. Named for Colonel Peter Gansevoort, a Revolutionary War hero, in 1837.

Gay Street—offically opened in 1833, it appears in the Common Council minutes for April 23, 1827 although it was not shown on any maps prior to 1823. In the late 1800's it was the site of one of the first black ghettos.

Germaine Street—former name of Carmine Street.

Glover Place—former name of Thompson St. between Prince and Spring Sts.

Great Jones Street—ceded to the city in 1806 by Samuel Jones, who was known as "the Father of the New York Bar"; not to be confused with Jones St., named after his wife's sister's husband, Dr. Gardiner Jones.

Great Kill Street or Road—former name for Gansevoort St. (q.v.); laid out prior to 1767 as a continuation of Fitzroy Road (Eighth Ave.)' see Gansevoort St.

Great Kiln Street—corruption of Great Kill (q.v.).

Greene Street—first called Union Street in 1794, then Second St. in the original numbering plan of city streets in 1794; it was named for Revolutionary War General Nathanael Greene in 1799. Greene St. was yet another street ceded to the city by Anthony L. Bleecker.

Greenwich Avenue—see Greenwich Lane.

Greenwich Lane—laid out in 1707 as a connection between the Hudson River and Bowery Road, it was closed between Broadway and Sixth Ave. in 1825 and between 13th St. and Eighth Ave. in 1826. It officially became Greenwich Ave. in 1843. (See also Art Street.)

Greenwich Street—although a road along the Hudson River was in use long before Admiral Sir Peter Warren bought his Greenwich property in 1744, this street was not officially laid out to the vicinity of Canal St. until 1739. It was not until 1808 that a cession by Trinity Church brought it from Brannon (Spring) past Christopher St.

Grove Street—supposedly named for the grove of trees near St. Luke's Church; see also Columbia, Cozine and Burrows Sts.

Hamersly Street—former name of part of West Houston St. running from Houstoun [sic] to West St., ceded to the city in 1808 by Trinity Church; became West Houston in 1858

Hamersly Place—former name of part of West Houston at the intersection of Hancock and Bedford Sts., it was obliterated along with Hancock when Sixth Ave. was run through in the 1920's.

Hammond Street—former name of West 11th St.

Hancock Street—seen now only by the buildings that once flanked its West Side, it was obliterated when Sixth Ave. was run through from Carmine to Canal Sts.

Carl Paler

The first house (pictured here in 1983) is typical of all frame houses in the Village at the turn of the Nineteenth Century. Directly behind is the servants' quarters which prior to and during the Civil War was a stop on the "underground railroad." Runaway slaves were housed here or in the series of "Slave Tunnels" that coursed under this portion of the Village (evidence of their existence was revealed during excavations here, on Christopher and West Tenth Street near Greenwich Avenue. It was probably here that Blacks were hidden from the raging mobs during the Draft Riots of 1863 (see History section). The third house, popularly known as "Twin Peaks" was originally a frame Federal house with pitched roof erected circa 1830. In 1925 Clifford Reed Dailey completely remodeled the structure into a pseudo-Medieval studio building. His concept of "inspiration for creative Villagers" was built along the lines of houses seen in Nuremberg Germany, It was funded by the wealthy patron of the arts, Otto Kahn.

The Gryphon of Twelfth Street.

The photo below was taken of the same grouping following the "restoration" completed in 1989 which attempted to return the front house to its original state. Actually there were several different configurations over the years as this building was built as two structures. The left-hand portion was built first and the right was added after 1822 probably to fill an existing yard. The combined buildings were then raised to three stories with one entrance on Grove Street--the configuration that we see below. Later it was returned to use as two residences with the federal doorway moved on Grove Street and another entrance added in the rear with the double windows in front added at a still later date. The "federal" doorway is new as are the clapboards on the Grove street facade and all windows are slightly smaller replacements. The clapboards on the Bedford side are original as is the entire "slave" house, now the oldest extant structure remaining in Greenwich Village. The Italianate cornice is from an 1850's upgrade. Sadly, the old half-moon shutters have been replaced (similar shutters can be seen across the street on Bedford Street near Christopher).

Typical of these reconstructions allowed by the Landmarks Preservation Commissions this building existed only briefly as it is seen today (another such travesty was permitted to be performed by a prominent doctor on the 18th Century commercial building on the corner of Bedford and Commerce), This tendency to force a "Williamsburg" type of conformity on a portion of New York that has never conformed as a whole, architecturally or spiritually, is decidedly unrealistic.

H. Kaplan   Carl Paler

Hazard Street—former name of King St.

Henry Street—original name of Perry St.

Herring Street—former name of Bleecker between Carmine and Bank Sts. and named for Robert Herring (Herinck), whose large holdings included all of the present Bleecker-Carmine Sts. area., Herring St. was laid out before 1799 and probably partially populated at that time. Early surveyors for the 1807-11 Commissioners Plan remarked on the variety of houses there in 1817 when it was run through to Amos (West 10th) St.

Hetty Street—original name of Charlton St.

Horatio Street—laid out prior to 1817 and officially opened from Greenwich to Hudson Sts. in 1834, it was named after General Horatio Gates, the Revolutionary Commander to whom General Burgoyne surrendered at Saratoga.

Houston (and West Houston) Street—laid out prior to 1797 as North St., it became Houstoun St. in 1808 when it was cut through to join Hamersly St. Nicholas Bayard III insisted it be named Houstoun when his daughter Mary married an often-elected delegate to the Continental Congress, William Houstoun. Although spelled correctly as "Houstoun" in Common council minutes for 1808 and on maps from 1811, by 1822 the street was almost universally referred to with its present-day spelling. Alas for some speculative historians, the street was neither named for Texan Sam Houston nor from the Dutch words *huys* and *tuyn* ("house garden"); God help any visitor foolish enough to say "Huustin" — everyone knows it should be pronounced "House-ton."

Hudson Street—laid out prior to 1797, it appears as far north as Greenwich Village by the time the State Prison was completed in 1798. It was regulated to Christopher St. in 1808 and formally opened to Ninth Ave. in 1817.

Jackson Square—a triangle bounded by Greenwich and Eighth Aves. and Horatio St., named after President Andrew Jackson; dedicated in 1826.

Jane Street—laid out prior to 1817 on land owned by the Jaynes family, who had occupied a house (The Bayard House) near No. 81 to which Alexander Hamilton was carried to die after his famous duel (see History). The name probably was corrupted to its present spelling when Jane Gahn (the ambitious daughter of John Ireland, a prominent land owner) owned and developed considerable property in the area.

Jones Street—named for Dr. Gardiner Jones; see Great Jones St.

King Street—laid out as Hazard St. prior to 1799, the name was later changed to honor Rufus King, a member of the Continental Congress; it was extended to the Hudson River in 1808.

LaGuardia Place—see Laurens St.

Laurens Street—laid out but not named prior to 1797, it was sometimes listed as Fourth St. under the old numbering system. It ramained Laurens St. until 1870 when Tammany Hall schemed to run Fifth Ave. through Washington Square Park to Canal Street and pushed through a bill to call it South Fifth Ave. This name lasted only a short time before being changed to West Broadway, which sticks to this day below West Houston — although recently it was renamed LaGuardia Place above West Houston north to Washington Square Park in honor of Fiorello LaGuardia, probably the most honest mayor New York City has had in recent times.

LeRoy Place—old name for Bleecker St. between Mercer and Greene Sts. in 1827, it was probably from the French *LeRoi*; LeRoy Place ceased to exist in 1878.

Leroy Street—named for Jacob Leroy, alderman and businessman, Leroy St. really consists of three streets joined together. Leroy St. proper (which was regulated from the Hudson River to the Episcopal churchyard by 1817) and Burton Street, which deadended on the other side of the churchyard (and began at Herring (Bleecker) St.), were both in place for 30 years prior to the sale of church property that allowed the third street, St. Luke's Place (q.v.), to be cut through. In 1845 the entire length became Leroy St., with numbering sequences blithely changing at Hudson St. to accommodate St. Luke's Place.

Locust Street—original name of Sullivan Street.

Lorillard Place—former name of Washington St. between Charles and Perry Sts.

MacDougal Street (and MacDougal Alley)—laid out well before 1799 as part of the West Bayard farm, it was regulated and named for Revolutionary Commander Alexander McDougall (whose father spelled the name MacDougal) in 1813. The portion between Waverly Place and West Fourth St. became Washington Square West in 1858.

Mercer Street—laid out prior to 1797 as Clermont Street and sometimes referred to as First St. under the old numbering system, it was named in honor of Hugh Mercer, an officer killed in the Revolutionary War.

McCarthy Square—a tiny triangle bounded by 7th Ave. South, Charles St. and Waverly Place, it was named in 1943 for Marine Private First Class Bernard Joseph McCarthy, killed on Guadalcanal in August 1942.

Milligan Place—built in 1848-49 along with nearby Patchin Place as a location for boarding houses for Basques employed at the Brevoort Hotel.

Milligan Street—laid out in 1805 on land owned by Samuel Milligan and surveyed by his future son-in-law Aaron D. Patchin, it became West 10th St. in 1811.

Minetta Lane—Minetta Street—Minetta Place—this tiny system of streets traces the course of the old Bestavaars Creek, or Minetta Brook, which ran across Washington Square and down Minetta Lane into Brook Street, thence into the Hudson near Charlton St. (see History). Minetta St. was once known as Brides' St. for the many millinery shops that thrived there.

Monument Lane-Road to the Obelisk—laid out prior to 1767 and declared a public road in 1786, this lane encompassed parts of the Sand Hill Road and Greenwich Lane from Bowery Lane to General Wolfe's obelisk at the corner of present-day Eighth Ave. and 14th St.

The old Mills Tavern, Bleecker Street.

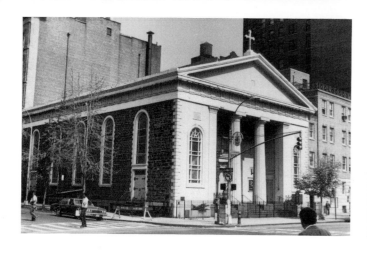

Left: St. Joseph's Church.
Right: St. Lukes in the Fields.
Lower left: Church of the Ascension.
Lower right: St. Veronica's, Christopher Street.

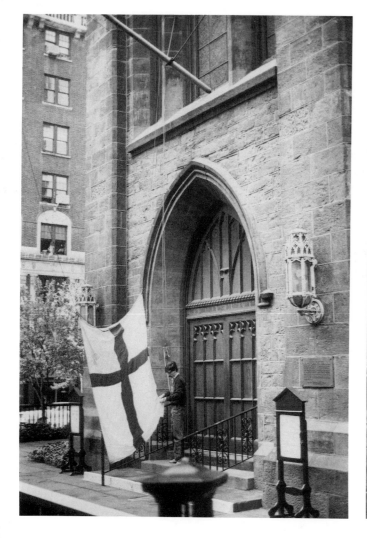

Before Seventh Avenue South made its nasty slash across the West Village, the tip of Sheridan Square as it intersected Grove was referred to as "the Mousetrap," a popular place to meet and trap your date.

Christopher Park (originally called Greenwich Park) once extended about ten yards further west. By 1848 when Asylum Street (West Fourth Street) (see Maps page 148) was run through, the park was reduced to its present dimensions.

Below and left opposite: The fence for Sheridan Square was cast in the exact dimensions of the 1836 fence around Christopher Park.

Sheridan Square was an empty triangular piece of pavement until the present garden was installed in 1984. Because no permanent structure had ever occupied the spot, a few enthusiasts decided that this might be an excellent area for an archaeological "dig" (in progress above). It netted very little except a few shards simply because Con Edison and other utilities had worked the site for nearly a hundred years before these neophytes got to it.

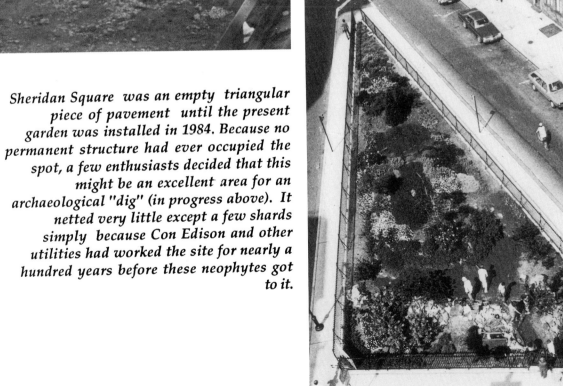

*C*hristopher Park was almost universally known as "Sheridan Square" since Seventh Avenue was put through in 1914 (see pages 27 and 116). Syd Brown made the same mistake when he produced the etching below in 1936, following a revitalization of the park. Adding to the confusion, The Sheridan Society erected this statue of General Philip Sheridan in Christopher Park at that time. The real Sheridan Square , a scant one block away, was named in 1890 for this General who is best (?) remembered for his declaration during the Western Campaigns: "The only good Indian I ever saw was dead."

Gaylord

SHERIDAN SQUARE
Syd Brown 36

135

Morton Street—laid out as Ardens Street prior to 1799, the name was changed in 1810 to honor Jacob Morton, a prominent lawyer. His street was originally where Clarkson St. now lies, but was moved two blocks north when the City Council needed a street to honor Matthew Clarkson, who outranked Morton—and therefore deserved a more honorable situation, next to Trinity Churchyard.

Ninth Avenue—opened from Greenwich Lane to 28th St. in 1815-16 along a former path from Chelsea House to Admiral Sir Peter Warren's house in Greenwich. Until just a few years ago the line of this path could be traced by the odd layout of backyards from 23rd to 14th Street.

North Street—laid out prior to 1799, when it was the northernmost finished street in Manhattan. It was extended to Broadway in 1806 and extended further to Hamersly St. in 1808 when the name was change to Houstoun (sic) St. (See Houston/West Houston Sts.)

Ogden Street—former name of Perry Street.

Patchin Place—named for Aaron D. Patchin; see Milligan St.

Perry Street—laid out prior to 1797 as Henry Street to follow the then-current vogue for naming streets with the first name of prominent landowners, its name was changed in 1799 to reflect the last name of Henry Ogden. Its present namesake is Commodore Oliver Hazard Perry, commander of the American Fleet in the Battle of Lake Erie during the War of 1812.

Prince Street—indicated but not named on an 1767 map, it officially became Rose St. in 1794 and acquired its present British royal name in 1813. Prince St. was the terminus of New York's first railway, which operated along Bowery Lane.

Prospect Street—original name of Thompson St.

Reason/Raisin Street—former names for Barrow St. (q.v.) between Herring (Bleecker) and Bedford Sts.

Rose Street—former name of Prince St.

Saint Lukes Place—named for the church on Hudson St.; see Leroy St.

Saint Marks Place—named for the church on the Bowery; see Eighth St.

Science Street—never more than a mapmaker's dream; see Art St.

Scott Street—former name of West 12th St.; after Francis Scott Key.

Below: Commerce Street, an etching by Georgia Chambers.
Right: West 12th Street.

Seventh Avenue South—laid out in the 1930's from Greenwich Ave. to Varick St.

Sheridan Square—up until 1983 a paved and barren triangle bounded by West Fourth and Barrow Sts. and Washington Place, Sheridan Square somehow missed being built upon, even during regulation of the adjoining streets during the period 1805-11. It is now the site of a handsome fenced park. Not to be confused with Christopher Park (where the statue of General Sheridan stands). (see Greenwich Park)

Sixth Avenue—opened from Greenwich Lane to Carmine St. in 1819, Sixth Ave. was extended to Canal St. in the 1920's for the Sixth Ave. Subway—obliterating Hancock and Congress Sts. and Hamersly Place.

Skinner Road—former name of Christopher St. (q.v.).

South Fifth Avenue—temporary name assigned to what is now LaGuardia Place, by a group of pirates headed by "Boss" Tweed shortly before his incarceration and death in Ludlow jail.

Spring Street—laid out prior to 1797 as Oliver St. to the east of Broadway and Brannon St. to the west, Spring St. has the dubious distinction of being possibly the only street in Manhattan named in reaction to the morbid curiosity of the general public. In 1800, Juliana Elmore Sands, a Quaker, was found drowned in a well fed by a natural spring near Broadway. The murder and accused killer, her sweetheart Levi Weeks, achieved such notoriety that the site was visited by hundreds of New Yorkers. Week's subsequent acquittal, engineered by the unlikely team of Aaron Burr and Alexander Hamilton, fueled such longterm excitement that guidebooks renamed the street Spring Street ("where *she* was murdered") long before the name became official in 1807.

Sullivan Street—laid out as Locust St. on the old West Bayard farm possibly as early as 1767, Sullivan St. was officially named for Revolutionary War hero Brigadier General John Sullivan in 1799.

Thompson Street—laid out as Prospect St. prior to 1797 on the old West Bayard Farm and sometimes referred to as Fifth Street under the *old* numbering system, its present name is a memorial to Revolutionary War Brigadier General William Thompson, who led a corps of sharpshooters from Pennsylvania in the defense of Boston after the Battle of Bunker Hill.

Union Square—recently "revitalized," this site of more mass rallies for more important causes than any other spot in New York is now knuckling under to gentrification—a dirty word which primarily suggests destruction, such as the destruction of the former S. Klein's group of 1860 buildings. Many more buildings in the area are threatened with demolition rather than restoration.

Tony Pastor's on Fourteenth Street in 1880. The infamous Tammany Hall (see History) was located to the left. Boss Tweed and Tammany Hall have become synonymous with corruption. The first Democratic convention in New York City was held here.

Gaylord

Near Left: The Mark Twain Home on West 10th Street.

Carl Paler

138

Patchin Place viewed from Sixth Avenue.

Carl Paler

Union Street—former name of Greene St.

University Place—named in 1858 for New York University, the first indication that the institution would try to take over the entire area; see Wooster St.

Vandam Street—named in 1807 for 19th-century Anthony Vandam, a descendant of Rip Vandam, the Albany-born Dutchman who was governor of the British Province of New York during 1731-32. Trinity Church ceded the extension of the street to the Hudson River in 1808.

Van Ness Place—former name of part of Charles Street from West Fourth to Bleecker St. (1866); named for Abraham Van Ness, who bought and occupied the Warren mansion in 1824, remembered by a tiny plaque at the corner of Christopher and 7th Ave. So.

Varick Street—opened in 1799 through land owned by Colonel Richard Varick, then mayor of New York City, it was extended to the Trinity churchyard at Houston St. in 1813 and now meets Seventh Ave. South at Carmine St.

Village Square—a tiny triangle bounded by Sixth Ave. and Christopher and West 10th Sts. soon to be named for Ruth Messinger, a village activist instrumental in saving Jefferson Market.

Washington Place—fromerly Fifth Street (under the present numbering system), which is interrupted in its run from Broadway to Sheridan Square by Washington Square Park. The extension beyond Sixth Ave. was at one time referred to as Upper or East Barrow St; it received its present name over its current length in 1833.

Washington Square—a quadrangle bounded by Washington Square North, East, South and West; see History and appropriate photo sections.

Washington Square North
Washington Square West
Washington Square East
Washington Square South.

Washington Street—*laid out in 1751 to Brannon (Spring) St.,* the land on which it now stands was not filled as far as Morton St. until 1810, and was not officially filled in and extended to the State Prison until 1813. Oddly enough, the land between Hammond (West 12th) St. and Fort Gansevoort was not filled in until 1851; Washington St. was completed, and Fort Gansevoort torn down, in that year, making way for Washington Market.

Below Left: An old stable building that once served as the block's fire house on Charles Street. Because of some strange city ordinance this structure has not been touched for almost fifty years.

Right: A stabilized piece on West Tenth Street.

Gaylord

G. Dahlberg

This is the oldest extant 19th Century shopfront building in the Village. It is located off Sixth Avenue at the terminus of MacDougal Street. It was built circa 1830 to serve the residents of Aaron Burr's project, now the Charlton, King, VanDam Historic District.

Carl Paler

Waverly Place (I)—formerly Sixth St. under the present numbering system, it was renamed in 1833 for Sir Walter Scott's popular novel *Waverly*. Admiring Villagers had petitioned the City Council for the name change.

Waverly Place (II)—formerly Factory St. between Christopher and Bank Sts., it had previous incarnations as Catherine and Eliza (for Eliza Fenno) Sts.; it was cut through to the other Waverly (see above) and given its present name in 1853, giving the triangular Northern Dispensary Building the unlikely distinction of being bounded on two sides by streets of the same name.

William Street (I)—former name for Asylum/West Fourth Sts., probably after William W. Gilbert.

William Street (II)—namesake unknown; former name for MacDougal St., laid out as early as 1767 on the old West Bayard farm.

Wooster Street—laid out (but not named) prior to 1797, it was sometimes referred to as Third St. under the old numbering system and carries the name of General David Wooster, killed in action in the Revolutionary War. It was extended to 14th St. in 1833, and parts of it were renamed Washington Square East and University Place in 1858. In a bold case of wholesale public thievery, New York University has blocked Wooster and Greene Sts. from public use between Washington Square and West Third St. with the aesthetically incompatible and disastrous Bobst Library. Wooster as well as Greene St. again blocked from puiblic Square Village, whose badly aging facades grow uglier and more out of place with each passing year. The University has just finished demolishing another group of historic structures to construct yet another alarmingly disproportionate building at the corner of MacDougal and West Third St.—13 stories of academic imperviousness to history, sitting on a block where the tallest dwelling is only six stories tall.

At right is a survey Map drawn in 1732 showing the division of Sir Peter Warren's Estate (see History Section). Note Greenwich Lane (the present Greenwich Avenue) and Skinner Road (Christopher Street). They had already been in place for fifty years,

MAPS
of NEW YORK CITY
showing the growth
of
GREENWICH
VILLAGE
from 1766 to present.

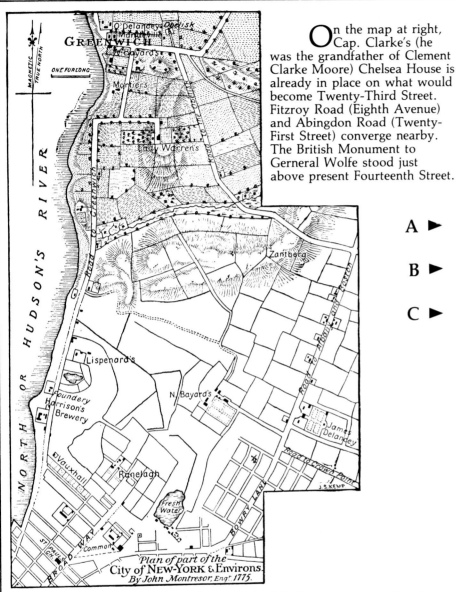

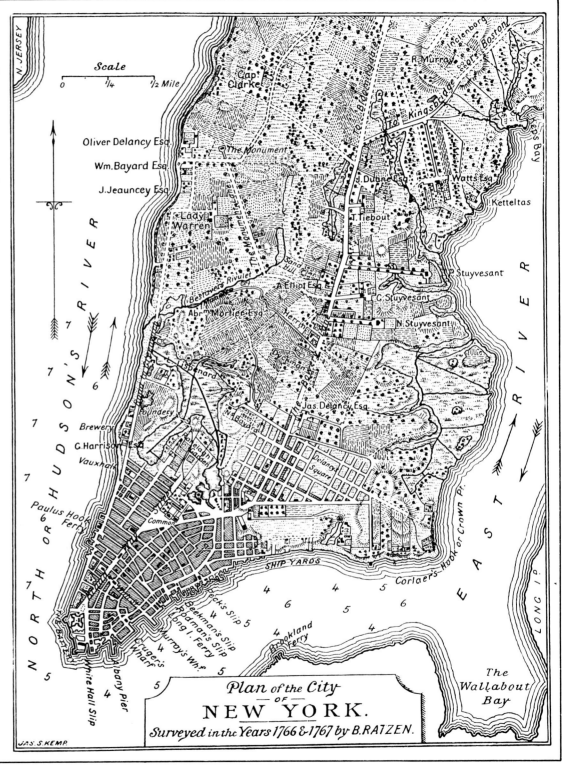

On the map at right, Cap. Clarke's (he was the grandfather of Clement Clarke Moore) Chelsea House is already in place on what would become Twenty-Third Street. Fitzroy Road (Eighth Avenue) and Abingdon Road (Twenty-First Street) converge nearby. The British Monument to Gerneral Wolfe stood just above present Fourteenth Street.

A ▶

B ▶

C ▶

As you can see, around 1770 lower Manhattan was a series of farms set among rolling hills and fresh water marshes. Greenwich Village was a small group of houses at the end of what is now Gansevoort Street, (at top of left-hand map near the word Greenwich) but the *entire area* was called "Greenwich".

Opposite letter A is Lady Warren's Greenwich House (Sir Peter was in England at this time). Letter B indicates the position of the foot of Christopher Street (then Skinner Road). If you look carefully for Elliot and Herring (opposite letter C) you will have located the future site of Washington Square. The Herring farm road from the Bowery Lane eventually became Bleecker Street and a portion of the Sand Hill road (just above) exists today as Astor Place.

The map below was drawn about 1783 and although it was purported to be "the latest map for all New York City", they obviously felt no need to include anything further north because there were still only a few houses and two tiny villages on the remainder of Manhattan Island. But as the map on the right shows the city rapidly expanded by 1803. The cause of this explosive activity was the ever increasing seriousness of the yellow fever epidemics, primarily the one in 1798.

There has always been some dispute about the exact boundaries of Greenwich Village and this map clarifies the argument. Greenwich Village was officially west of Broadway (because up to the 1820's to the east was open farm land) and north of the culvert that ran down to Collect Pond (approximately Spring Street) and south of the original village of Sapokanikanee at Gansvoort Street. Number 34 on the References list at right is the State Prison at the foot of West Tenth Street.

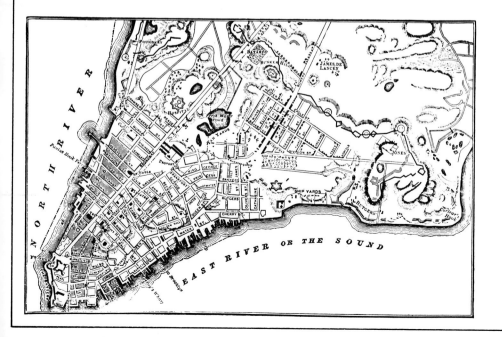

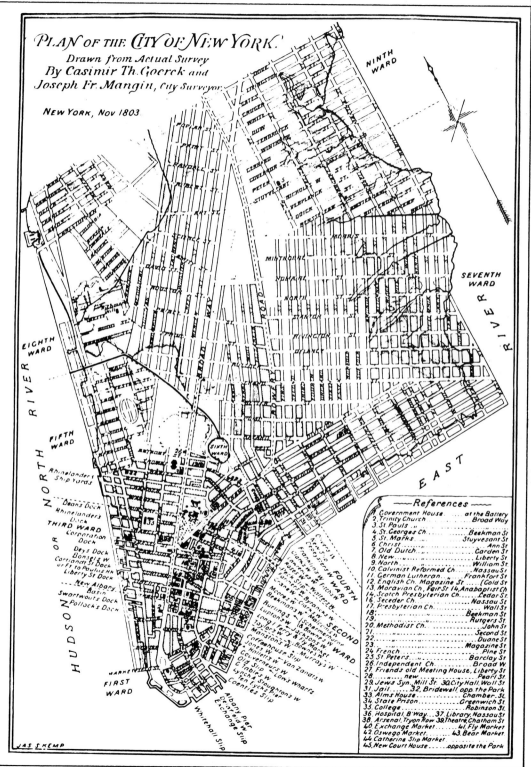

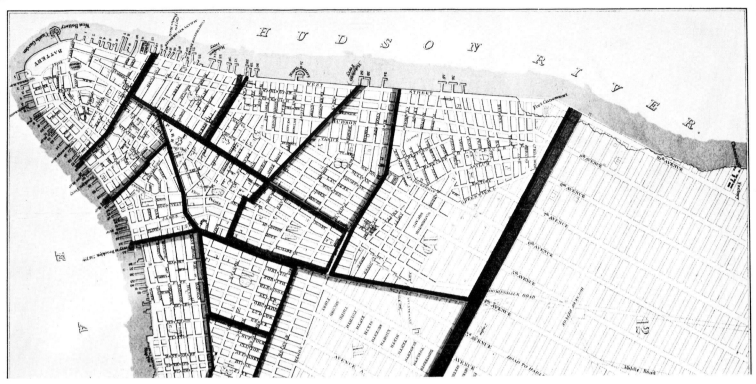

By 1848 when the map at top was drawn by William Hooker, Greenwich Village as we know it today was mostly in place. The shaded blocks were completely populated although some areas all the way to 42nd Street were built up. Note the growth by 1851 on the following map by Valentine.

The bottom map shows a view of the Village in 1822 following the Yellow Fever Epidemic of that year. The list at the top shows all the important institutions that were located in the Village. Note the prominence of the State Prison in 1822, and the tiny building indicated on the map at right.

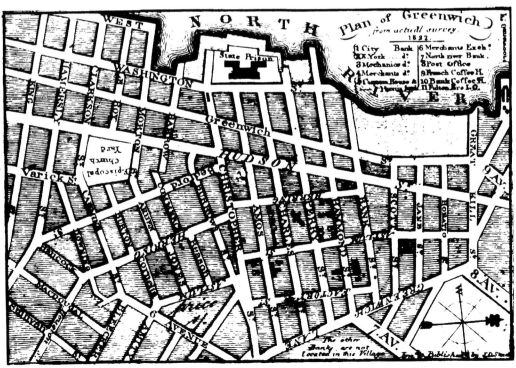

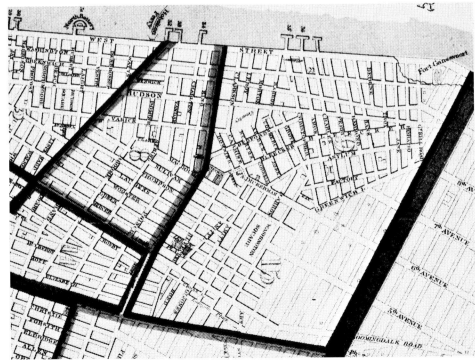

On the following page, this map from 1905 shows the Village during the heyday of the Ocean Liners. None of the Avenues have been run through and the Village remains isolated. The black lines indicate Elevated Lines or tramways and the Lexington Avenue Subway stops were indicated by the large black dots. Note that a ferry ran to the foot of Christopher Street and the Path tunnel to New Jersey had stops at Christopher and Ninth Streets.

By 1851 the city had grown past 42nd Street and the shore line had been filled in to West Street. In the Village the State Prison has been torn down as well as Fort Gansvoort.

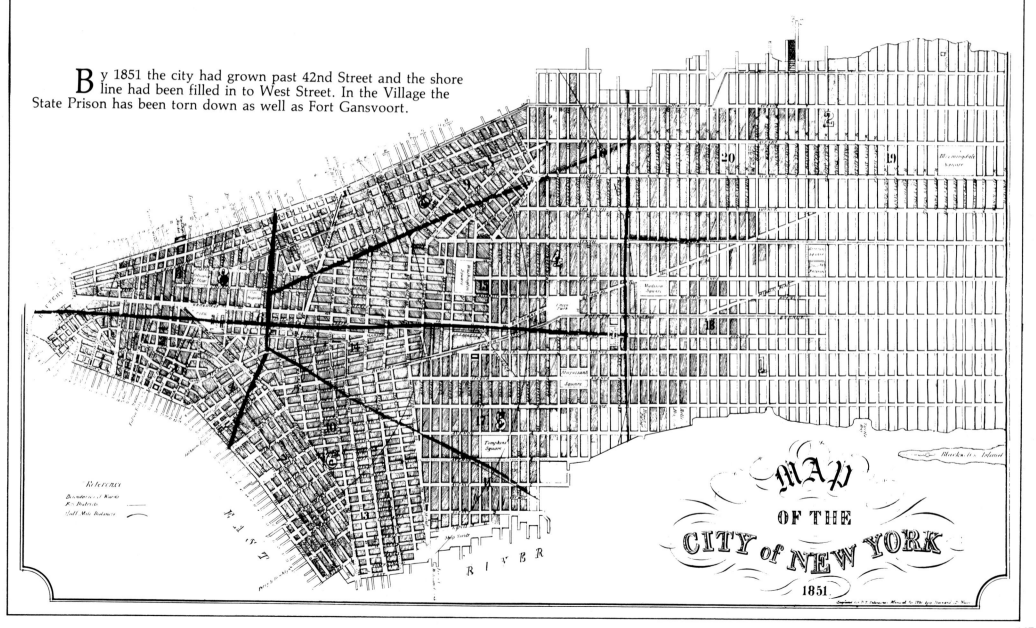

MAP
OF THE
CITY of NEW YORK
1851

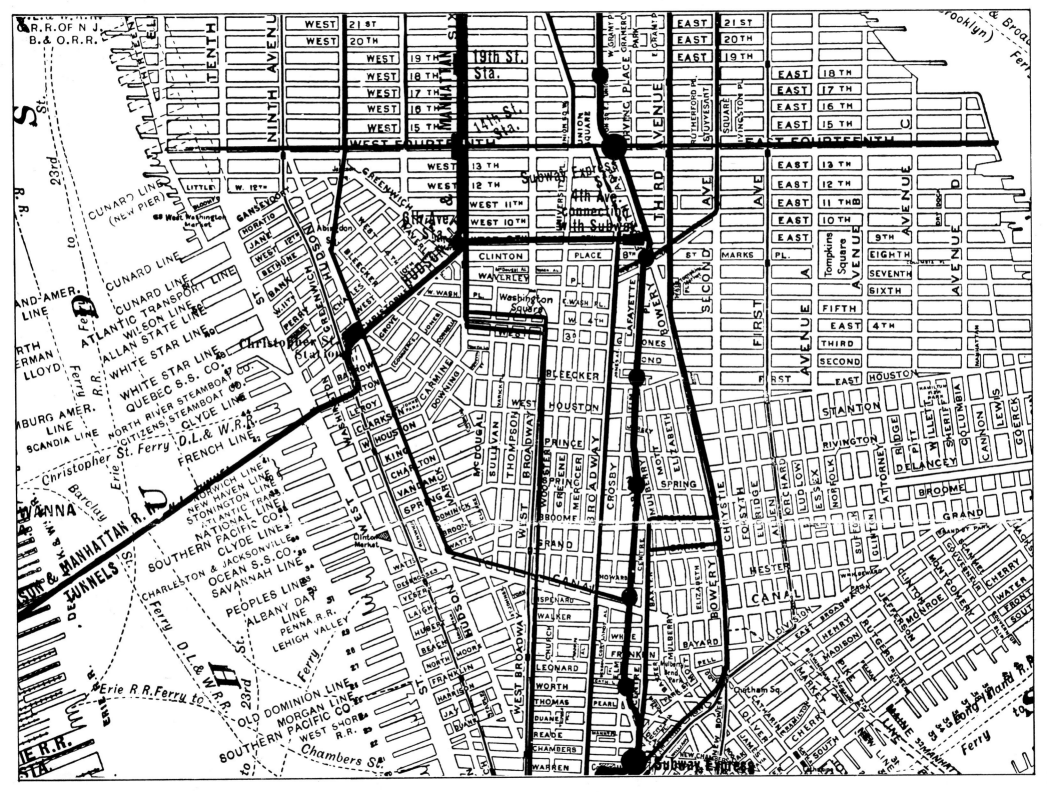

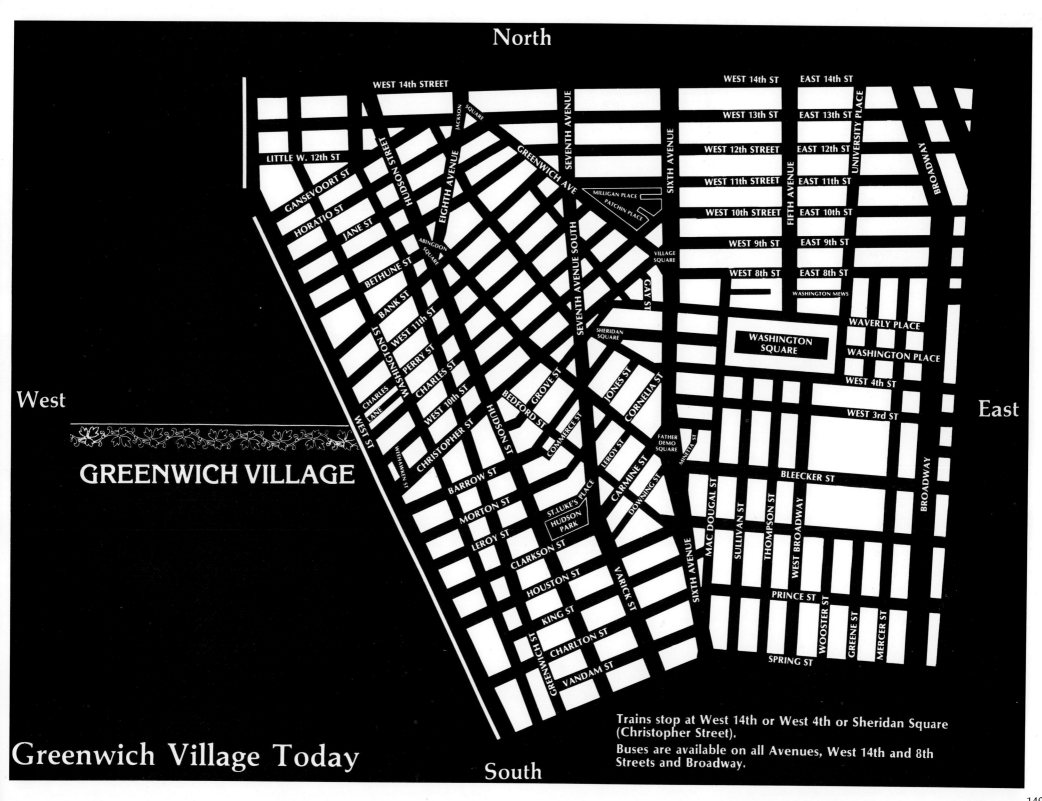

North

West

East

South

West 14th STREET · WEST 14th ST · EAST 14th ST

JACKSON SQUARE · WEST 13th ST · EAST 13th ST

LITTLE W. 12th ST · WEST 12th STREET · EAST 12th ST

GANSEVOORT ST · GREENWICH AVE · WEST 11th STREET · EAST 11th ST

HORATIO ST · HUDSON STREET · EIGHTH AVENUE · SEVENTH AVENUE · SIXTH AVENUE · MILLIGAN PLACE · PATCHIN PLACE · WEST 10th STREET · EAST 10th ST

JANE ST · ABINGDON SQUARE · WEST 9th ST · EAST 9th ST

BETHUNE ST · VILLAGE SQUARE · WEST 8th ST · EAST 8th ST

BANK ST · SEVENTH AVENUE SOUTH · WASHINGTON MEWS

WEST 11th ST · WASHINGTON ST · GAY ST · WAVERLY PLACE

PERRY ST · CHARLES LANE · SHERIDAN SQUARE · WASHINGTON SQUARE · WASHINGTON PLACE

CHARLES ST · WEST 4th ST

WEST 10th ST · JONES ST · CORNELIA ST · WEST 3rd ST

CHRISTOPHER ST · BEDFORD ST · GROVE ST · COMMERCE ST · LEROY ST · FATHER DEMO SQUARE · MINETTA ST

WEEHAWKEN ST · HUDSON STREET · CARMINE ST · BLEECKER ST

BARROW ST · DOWNING ST

MORTON ST · CARMINE ST · MAC DOUGAL ST · SULLIVAN ST · THOMPSON ST · WEST BROADWAY · BROADWAY

LEROY ST · ST. LUKE'S PLACE · HUDSON PARK · SIXTH AVENUE

CLARKSON ST · PRINCE ST · WOOSTER ST · GREENE ST · MERCER ST

HOUSTON ST · VARICK ST · SPRING ST

KING ST · WEST ST

CHARLTON ST · GREENWICH ST

VANDAM ST

FIFTH AVENUE · UNIVERSITY PLACE · BROADWAY

GREENWICH VILLAGE

Trains stop at West 14th or West 4th or Sheridan Square (Christopher Street).

Buses are available on all Avenues, West 14th and 8th Streets and Broadway.

Greenwich Village Today

INDEX

All Named Streets are in alphabetical order in the Street Section, Page 125.
Check Authors Section for the complete list of authors, Page 70.

Newsboys near the park in 1895.
Photo M. Cohen courtesy of Joe Coppa.

A

B

H. Kaplan

Almost invisible from Charles Street, Pottery Heaven is typical of the many artist studios which once existed in the basements of the West Village. A one woman show of her own, Rona Texidor produces one-of-kind creations in clay.

C

D

E

F

G

The pineapple was a symbol of welcome in the early days of our nation. This particular one is on West 11th Street just where it crosses West Fourth Street (an anomoly that occurrs only in Greenwich Village). This symbol may also be seen on the knewel posts of three houses on MacDougal Street near West Third that were built by Aaron Burr in 1827.

Steven Bloomfield

P

Q

R

S

Village Halloween, 1990

T

Gaylord

Laura Leeds